IGNITE

IGNITE

~~~~~~

101 TIPS & HACKS TO START AND SCALE YOUR BUSINESS

Frank O'Grady

INTRODUCTION

Having been involved in many startups and small to medium businesses over the years, I found that they often face very similar challenges. Verbatim almost. It can be very hard for a small business owner, often with limited resources, to keep on top of so many areas when starting and scaling a company. This makes no real difference if the company is B2B (Business to Business) or B2C (Business to Consumer). Or whether you produce a product or a service.

This book is intended to give a helicopter view of some of the key challenges that entrepreneurs and small business owners face and how to deal with them. A few good habits chucked in for good measure, and where possible presented in a list format so it should hopefully be easy to digest.

With some luck you will find it useful and it may help you deal with these challenges, better strategize, avoid some of the inevitable disasters, save some valuable time, or even generate new revenue.

If you find that just 2 or 3 these pointers help you in your ability to deal with the day-to-day grind or maybe a particular challenge you are facing, then I believe it will have been of real value. Some of the smallest habits that I have taken up over the last 20 years, have had had the most profound impact. From something simple such as checking email no more than twice a day (ideally once) to developing a systematic approach to work in general.

Feel free to make notes wherever you find points of particular interest and remember that building a business and plugging the inevitable holes in skillsets, is largely often about habit forming as it is anything else. There is rarely a quick fix so be prepared to apply yourself, and over time you should see real and quantifiable progress.

CONTENTS

CHAPTER

1

TAKING THE LEAP

STARTING OUT CAN BE A RISKY BUSINESS

LEAVING THE 9 TO 5 to start a company is not for the faint hearted. Do you know why are you doing this? Is it your passion? Necessity may be mother of invention, but it is crucial that you enjoy what you do. I personally enjoy the process. Know your own strengths and weaknesses, likes and dislikes. Self-awareness is a great asset. Before taking the leap into entrepreneurship and leaving your job to start a business, it's important to consider several key factors to ensure a smooth transition and increase your chances of success:

Financial stability: Evaluate your financial situation and determine if you have enough savings or a backup plan to sustain yourself during the initial stages of your business when revenue might be limited. Prepare a financial cushion to cover personal and business expenses until your venture becomes profitable.

Business viability: Thoroughly research and validate your business idea to ensure its potential for success. Assess the market demand, competition, and potential profitability of your product or service. Conduct market research, seek feedback from potential customers, and create a comprehensive business plan.

Skillset and expertise: Assess your skills and expertise in relation to the requirements of your business. Identify any gaps and determine if you need additional training or resources to succeed. Consider whether you have the necessary industry knowledge and experience to navigate challenges and make informed decisions.

Support network: Evaluate your support system, including family, friends, mentors, and business networks. Surround yourself with people who believe in your vision and can offer guidance, advice, and emotional support. Building a strong network can be invaluable during the ups and downs of starting a business.

Work-life balance: Reflect on your personal priorities and how starting a business might affect your work-life balance. Understand that entrepreneurship often requires long hours, dedication, and sacrifices. Consider the impact on your personal relationships, health, and overall well-being.

Legal and regulatory considerations: Familiarize yourself with the legal and regulatory requirements for starting and operating a business in your industry and location. Ensure you have the necessary licenses, permits, and comply with tax obligations. Consult with legal and financial professionals to navigate these complexities.

Exit strategy: Have a clear exit strategy in mind. Consider what will happen if your business doesn't succeed as planned. Determine if you would be willing to return to a traditional job or explore other opportunities.

Can you get your business off the ground without financial help from friends or family? Personally, it would never sit well with me owing friends or family but each to their own.

By carefully considering these factors, you can make informed decisions, mitigate risks, and set yourself up for a successful transition from employment to entrepreneurship.

1   *Ask yourself why are you doing this?*

UNLEASHING CREATIVITY: HOW TO COME UP WITH A GOOD BUSINESS IDEA

In today's fast-paced and competitive world, having a unique and innovative business idea is essential for success. However, generating such ideas can be a daunting task. Let's look at some strategies and practical tips to ignite your creativity and help you come up with a good business idea.

1. Identify Your Passions and Interests

    Start by exploring your passions and interests. What activities excite you? What problems do you find yourself trying to solve? Consider your hobbies, skills, and knowledge areas. Passion fuels motivation and aligning your business idea with your interests increases your chances of success. Take time to reflect on what truly inspires you, as this will form the foundation for a unique and fulfilling venture.

2. Conduct Market Research

    Once you have identified your interests, delve into market research to understand existing gaps, trends, and potential opportunities. Analyse consumer needs, preferences, and pain points in the relevant industry. Study your competition to identify areas where you can differentiate yourself. Market research will provide valuable insights into market demand, target audience, and potential market size, helping you refine your business idea and position it effectively.

3. Solve a Problem

Great businesses are built on the premise of solving problems. Look for challenges or inefficiencies in everyday life or specific industries. Consider how you can provide a solution that improves people's lives or simplifies existing processes. A problem-solving mindset ensures that your business idea has practical relevance and addresses real needs, making it more likely to gain traction and attract customers.

4. Brainstorm and Ideation

Create an environment conducive to brainstorming and ideation. Surround yourself with diverse perspectives, collaborate with others, and encourage free thinking. Brainstorming sessions can take various forms, such as mind mapping, SWOT analysis, or concept association. Use these techniques to generate a wide range of ideas, without self-judgment. Capture all ideas, no matter how unusual they may seem, as they can serve as a springboard for refining and evolving your business concept.

5. Prototype and Validate

Transform your ideas into tangible prototypes or minimum viable products (MVPs). A prototype can be a physical product, a digital mock-up, or a service outline. Test your concept with potential customers, gather feedback, and iterate based on their input. Validating your idea early on helps identify potential flaws, understand customer preferences, and refine your business model. This iterative process allows you to fine-tune your idea before investing significant time and resources into its implementation.

Coming up with a good business idea requires a combination of creativity, market awareness, and problem-solving skills. By aligning your passions with market demand, conducting thorough research, and fostering a collaborative ideation process, you can increase the likelihood of generating an innovative and successful business idea. Remember, persistence, adaptability, and continuous learning are key to transforming your idea into a thriving venture.

3 *Try to solve a problem. Make a habit of regularly identifying problems. This might spark something.*

PASSION OVER PROFIT

This cannot be overemphasised enough. Going out on your own in business can be life changing so it is CRUCIAL that you have real passion for what it is that you do. People who are driven by money don't always end up making money. If you have passion for what you do the revenue will often come as a by-product. Passion plays a crucial role when starting a business as it can provide several significant advantages and contribute to long-term success for a variety of reasons:

1. Motivation and Perseverance: Starting and running a business can be challenging, and there will be obstacles and setbacks along the way. Passion fuels motivation and keeps entrepreneurs driven during difficult times. When you are genuinely passionate about your business idea, you are more likely to persevere, overcome obstacles, and stay committed to your goals.

2. Energy and Enthusiasm: Passion generates a contagious energy and enthusiasm that can attract others to your business. Whether it's investors, customers, or team members, people are often drawn to individuals who genuinely believe in what they are doing. Your passion can inspire others to join your journey and support your vision.

3. Innovation and Creativity: Passion often leads to a deep understanding and knowledge of your industry or field. This knowledge, combined with a genuine interest and enthusiasm, can spark innovative ideas and creative solutions. Passionate entrepreneurs are more likely to think outside the box, challenge traditional approaches, and come up with unique and disruptive business models.

4. Resilience and Adaptability: The entrepreneurial journey is filled with uncertainty and constant changes. Passionate entrepreneurs are more likely to adapt to evolving market conditions, industry trends, and customer needs. They are willing to learn, pivot when necessary, and embrace new opportunities. Passion provides the resilience needed to navigate through uncertainties and adapt to the ever-changing business landscape.

5. Customer Connection: Passionate entrepreneurs deeply care about their customers and their needs. This genuine concern helps build strong connections and relationships with customers. When you are passionate about solving a problem or meeting a need, you are more likely to understand your customers' pain points, empathize with them, and provide exceptional products or services that truly address their needs.

6. Personal Fulfilment: Starting a business based on your passion allows you to align your work with your values, interests, and talents. It gives you the opportunity to pursue something meaningful and fulfilling. When you enjoy what you do, it positively impacts your overall well-being and satisfaction, contributing to a sense of fulfilment in your entrepreneurial journey.

7. Long-Term Commitment: Entrepreneurship requires dedication and long-term commitment. Passion sustains your commitment to your business over the long haul. It helps you stay engaged, motivated, and invested in the growth and success of your venture, even during challenging times.

While passion is important, it's essential to balance it with a solid business strategy, market research, and financial planning. Passion alone cannot guarantee business success, but when combined with strategic thinking, careful planning, and continuous learning, it can be a powerful driving force behind entrepreneurial endeavours.

VALIDATION – THE MOST IMPORTANT STAGE IN STARTING A BUSINESS

As you start working on your business you will come to the MOST critical of stages - validation. Validation is where you prove there is a market for your product. That may be getting pre orders for your product or service, that may be creating a beta product and getting actual customers on board. Ultimately it is getting somebody to pay for what you do. And ideally, getting several people to pay.

This will potentially fast track investment into your business if required. And if your business doesn't require investment, it'll fast track the organic growth of your business. It will also help identify marketing strategies to scale your business.

4 *Validation is THE MOST important step in starting a business. It proves you have a saleable product or service and de-risks any investment hugely*

Validating a new business is a crucial step in ensuring its potential success and minimizing risks. By thoroughly assessing your business idea and conducting market research, you can gather valuable insights that will inform your decision-making and help you refine your strategy. Some key steps to effectively validate your business:

1. Define your target audience: Clearly identify who your potential customers are. Understand their needs, preferences, and pain points. This will guide you in tailoring your product or service to meet their specific demands.

2. Conduct market research: Analyse the market landscape to assess competition, market size, and growth potential. Identify any gaps or opportunities that your business can capitalize on. Explore existing alternatives and determine how your offering stands out.

3. Test your value proposition: Develop a clear value proposition that communicates the unique benefits your business provides. Test it with your target audience through surveys, focus groups, or interviews. Assess their reactions and refine your value proposition based on their feedback.

4. Create a minimum viable product (MVP): Build a prototype or minimum viable product to demonstrate your business concept. This allows you to test your idea in the market and gather user feedback to identify areas for improvement. Iterate and refine your MVP based on user insights.

5. Seek early adopters: Identify early adopters within your target audience who are willing to try your product or service. Offer them incentives or discounts in exchange for feedback. Their experiences and testimonials can serve as social proof and attract more customers.

6. Analyse financial viability: Assess the financial feasibility of your business idea. Calculate costs, pricing, and projected revenue. Consider factors such as overhead expenses, production costs, and potential sales volume. Ensure that your business model is sustainable and profitable.

7. Monitor industry trends: Stay up to date with industry trends, emerging technologies, and customer behaviours. Adapt your business strategy accordingly to remain relevant and competitive.

8. Seek expert advice: Consult with industry experts, mentors, or advisors who can provide valuable insights and guidance. Their experience can help you avoid common pitfalls and refine your business model.

9. GET SALES. The absolute most important proof that you are on to something. Get actual sales or at the very least pre orders.

By following these steps, you can validate your new business idea more effectively and increase your chances of building a successful venture. Remember, the validation process is iterative, and continuous learning and adaptation are key to long-term success.

If you're seeking seed investment pre validation and you're very early in your business cycle, you may end up having to give up a substantial chunk of your company for small amount of capital. But then if you put that money to good use and grow the business you may have a follow-on funding round at a much more significant valuation. In general, though it would be recommended to look at funding post validation.

VALIDATION DE–RISKS INVESTMENT AND DRIVES UP THE VALUE OF THE BUSINESS.

THINGS YOU NEED TO CONSIDER

PROFITIBILITY - Understand this - What's the gross margin of your product or service? – Your profit as a % of your sales. What's it costing you to produce the product or service for your customers? Ideally, you want as high a gross margin as possible. Gross Profit is an important financial indicator for assessing a company's profitability and operational efficiency. A higher gross profit margin indicates that a company generates more profit per dollar of revenue, which can be an indication of strong pricing strategies, effective cost management, or a competitive advantage in the market.

To calculate gross profit, you need to follow these steps:

1. Determine Total Revenue: This refers to the total amount of revenue generated from the sale of goods or services during a specific period. It can include sales revenue from products, services, or any other sources of income.

2. Calculate Cost of Goods Sold (COGS): COGS represents the direct costs associated with producing or acquiring the goods or services that were sold. It typically includes the cost of raw materials, direct labour, and any manufacturing or production expenses. If you are a service-based company, the COGS may include the direct costs associated with providing the service.

3. Subtract COGS from Total Revenue: Subtract the COGS from the total revenue to calculate the gross profit. The formula is as follows:
   Gross Profit = Total Revenue - Cost of Goods Sold
   Gross Margin = Gross Profit as % of sales

The resulting figure represents the gross profit, which is the amount of profit generated by the company's core operations before considering other expenses such as overhead costs, taxes, and interest payments.

Gross profit is a crucial metric as it helps assess a company's ability to generate profits from its direct operations. It provides insights into the efficiency of the production or acquisition of goods or services and the pricing strategies employed by the company.

It's important to note that gross profit alone does not provide a comprehensive view of a company's overall financial performance. It is often analysed in conjunction with other financial metrics, such as net profit margin, to assess the profitability and efficiency of the business.

BUSINESS PLAN

I recommend that anyone starting a business should create a Business Plan. A Business Plan will address things such as;

- FOCUS? A business plan will give you focus and highlight potential issues.
- SWOT Analysis list Strengths Weakness Opportunities and threats
- MARKET - Look at the Landscape, Competition etc.
- FINANCIALS – If you are looking to bring an investor on board, at some stage they are going to want to get a return and ideally an exit. Realistically five yrs. but often ten or more

OFFICE SPACE

Do you need office space? There may be shared incubation spaces in your area. Go online and see what sort of start-up facilities there are out there. Maybe can get a two three-man office that's subsidised by local councils or government, and you have additional benefits of networking with similar companies on a similar journey.

DO THOROUGH ANALYSIS

Do not go asking friends or family. Do proper research. Nothing beats shoe leather, pick up the phone, ring potential customers, ring friends that may know potential customers, but get some feedback from people in the industry as to whether or not there is a demand for your product or service. Look at existing competition. Are they falling short? Is the quality not that great or is there an opportunity based on price? What is it that makes you believe there is a market for your product or service? This is important. In any process, you have your stages of analysis, development and testing and a business is no different. The analysis stage is critical. Too often in the business startup processes, the analysis stage is not done thoroughly enough. This could have a massive impact on your business. Because if you've spent time and effort building something and hasn't been analysed properly from the outset, your product won't meet customer needs and you'll end up with a huge amount of adjusting to do down the line, which will only end up costing time and money.

If that means picking up the phone and asking somebody for 10 minutes of their time to present a business idea you're working on to them, do it. Could they meet you for coffee? There's nothing to be lost by picking up the phone. The worst thing that can happen is they won't take your call, or they won't meet you. But in business there is really no replacement for graft. For hustle. You must be able to do the grind, make the difficult calls, put in the hard work, put in the 12-hour days if needed and in the analysis stage, it's critically important.

 **Research and then research some more. You can never do too much research at the outset.**

FUNDRAISING – HOW MUCH, WHERE and WHEN

When starting a business, securing adequate funding is essential to cover initial expenses, invest in resources, and facilitate growth. Here are several ways to raise money for your new venture:

1. Personal savings: Utilize your personal savings to fund your business. This approach allows you to maintain full control over your business and avoid debt or external obligations.

2. Family and friends: It is here as it is an option that many go to first. It must be noted though that it is NOT one though I would ever recommend. You can though present your business idea and seek investments or loans from family members and friends who believe in your vision. Be clear about repayment terms and ensure transparency to maintain healthy relationships.

7

Even though it is listed here as an option I HIGHLY ADVISE do not raise money from friends or family.

3. Crowdfunding: Platforms like Kickstarter, Indiegogo, and GoFundMe enable you to raise funds from a large number of individuals. Create a compelling campaign, set rewards for different contribution levels, and leverage social media to spread the word about your project.

4. Small Business Grants: Research and apply for small business grants provided by government agencies, nonprofit organizations, or corporations. These grants often have specific eligibility criteria, so ensure that your business aligns with their requirements.

5. Bank loans: Approach financial institutions for business loans. Prepare a solid business plan, financial projections, and collateral to increase your chances of approval. Explore different loan options, such as Small Business Administration (SBA) loans, which are specifically designed for small businesses.

6. Angel investors: Angel investors are individuals or groups who provide capital to startups in exchange for equity or convertible debt. They often offer expertise and mentorship in addition to funding. Network with angel investor groups, attend startup events, and pitch your business to attract potential investors.

7. Venture capital: Venture capital firms invest in high-growth startups with significant potential. They provide funding in exchange for equity and are often involved in strategic

decision-making. To secure venture capital funding, develop a strong business plan, demonstrate scalability, and highlight your unique selling points.

8. Bootstrapping: Start and grow your business with minimal external funding. Focus on generating revenue from the early stages, reinvest profits into the business, and carefully manage expenses. This approach allows you to maintain control and retain a larger share of your business.

Consider a combination of these funding methods to diversify your sources and reduce risk. Each option has its own advantages and considerations, so choose the approach that aligns best with your business goals, financial needs, and growth plans.

SYSTEMS - START WITH A SYSTEMATIC APPROACH

Having a systematic approach to business is crucial for achieving efficiency, consistency, and long-term success. It provides structure, clarity, and a framework for decision-making. Sp why is a systematic approach so important?:

Efficiency: A systematic approach allows businesses to streamline processes, eliminate redundancy, and optimize resource allocation. By establishing clear workflows and standard operating procedures, you can reduce errors, minimize waste, and improve productivity. This leads to cost savings, improved customer satisfaction, and increased profitability.

8   *A Systematic Approach is KEY.*

Consistency: Consistency is vital for building a strong brand and delivering a high-quality customer experience. A systematic approach ensures that every aspect of your business, from operations to customer service, follows established protocols and meets defined standards. This consistency builds trust, enhances reputation, and fosters customer loyalty.

Scalability: A systematic approach facilitates scalability by creating a framework that can be replicated and expanded as the business grows. It allows for efficient onboarding of new employees, easier delegation of tasks, and seamless integration of new processes or technologies. This scalability enables businesses to adapt to increasing demand, enter new markets, and seize growth opportunities.

Decision-making: A systematic approach provides a structured framework for decision-making. It enables businesses to gather and analyse data, assess risks, and evaluate options systematically. This helps in making informed decisions based on objective criteria rather than relying on guesswork or intuition. By following a systematic approach, businesses can reduce the likelihood of costly mistakes and make strategic choices that align with their goals.

Adaptability: In a rapidly changing business landscape, adaptability is crucial. A systematic approach enables businesses to respond to market shifts, customer preferences, and emerging trends with agility. By having structured processes and a clear understanding of the business's strengths and weaknesses, you can pivot, innovate, and seize new opportunities.

A systematic approach to business is essential for driving efficiency, consistency, and sustainable growth. It empowers businesses to optimize operations, make informed decisions, and adapt to changing circumstances. By embracing a systematic mindset, businesses can enhance performance, maximize competitiveness, and achieve long-term success.

Continuous improvement: A systematic approach fosters a culture of continuous improvement within the organization. By regularly evaluating processes, gathering feedback, and measuring key performance indicators, businesses can identify areas for enhancement and implement changes. This iterative approach allows for ongoing optimization, innovation, and adaptation to changing market dynamics.

KPIs (KEY PERFORMANCE INDICATORS):

Key Performance Indicators (KPIs) are essential in business for several reasons:

1. Goal alignment: KPIs help align the organization's goals with its overall strategy. They provide a clear focus on what is most important to achieve success, ensuring that everyone within the organization is working towards the same objectives.

2. Measurement and evaluation: KPIs enable businesses to measure and evaluate their performance against

predetermined targets. They provide quantifiable metrics that can be tracked over time, allowing companies to assess their progress and identify areas of improvement or success.

3. Performance monitoring: KPIs act as a monitoring tool to keep track of critical activities, processes, and outcomes. By regularly monitoring these indicators, businesses can identify potential issues or bottlenecks early on, enabling them to take corrective action promptly.

4. Decision-making: KPIs provide valuable insights that facilitate data-driven decision-making. When properly defined and tracked, KPIs offer a factual basis for evaluating the success of various initiatives, projects, or strategies. This helps business leaders make informed decisions and prioritize resources effectively.

5. Accountability and transparency: KPIs establish accountability within an organization by setting clear expectations and performance standards. They create a framework for employees to understand what is expected of them and provide a basis for performance evaluations. Additionally, transparently sharing KPIs and performance results fosters trust and engagement among stakeholders.

6. Continuous improvement: KPIs promote a culture of continuous improvement by encouraging businesses to analyse their performance and identify opportunities for growth. By regularly reviewing KPIs and benchmarking against industry standards or competitors, organizations can identify best practices, implement changes, and drive innovation.

7. Communication and alignment: KPIs serve as a communication tool, ensuring that everyone in the

organization understands what needs to be achieved and how their efforts contribute to overall success. They facilitate better coordination between departments, teams, and individuals, fostering collaboration and alignment towards shared goals.

Overall, KPIs are essential in business because they provide a framework for goal setting, performance evaluation, decision-making, and continuous improvement. They help organizations stay focused, monitor progress, and drive success in a measurable and transparent manner.

9   Set KPIs as part of your daily tasks.

NOTES

CHAPTER

2

THE BUSINESS PLAN & PITCH DECK

A BUSINESS PLAN PLAYS a crucial role when starting a business as it serves as a roadmap for success. It is a comprehensive document that outlines the goals, strategies, and financial projections of a business. Preparing one might take a bit of time but some of the many benefits include:

1. Clarifies Business Objectives: A business plan forces entrepreneurs to clearly define their business objectives, mission, and vision. It helps answer fundamental questions about what the business aims to achieve, its target market, and the products or services it will offer. This clarity of purpose provides a strong foundation for making informed decisions and setting realistic goals.

2. Guides Decision-Making: A well-written business plan acts as a guide for decision-making at every stage of the business. It helps entrepreneurs evaluate different opportunities, assess potential risks, and make informed choices. By outlining strategies, market analysis, and financial projections, a business plan helps in weighing the pros and cons of various options, allowing entrepreneurs to make informed decisions that align with their long-term vision.

3. Attracts Investors and Financing: When seeking funding or investment for a business, a solid business plan is essential. Investors and lenders want to see a well-thought-out plan that demonstrates the potential for profitability and growth. A business plan that includes a clear market analysis, competitive advantage, and financial projections enhances the credibility of the business and increases the likelihood of securing financing.

4. Sets Realistic Expectations: A business plan requires entrepreneurs to conduct thorough market research and feasibility analysis. This process helps in setting realistic expectations about the market demand, competition, and potential challenges. By identifying potential obstacles and developing contingency plans, entrepreneurs are better prepared to navigate unforeseen circumstances and adapt their strategies accordingly.

5. Facilitates Operational Efficiency: A business plan outlines the organizational structure, operational processes, and resource requirements of the business. It helps identify the key activities, timelines, and responsibilities required for successful execution. By establishing clear objectives and performance indicators, a business plan enables entrepreneurs to monitor progress, identify areas for improvement, and ensure operational efficiency.

6. Supports Growth and Expansion: As the business evolves, a business plan acts as a roadmap for growth and expansion. It helps entrepreneurs identify opportunities for diversification, new market segments, or additional products/services. By regularly reviewing and updating the business plan, entrepreneurs can evaluate the business's performance, adapt strategies, and capitalize on emerging trends or market shifts.

7. Provides a Communication Tool: A well-crafted business plan serves as a communication tool to share the business's vision, strategies, and goals with stakeholders, including employees, partners, and potential investors. It aligns everyone involved in the business and provides a clear

understanding of the business's direction, fostering collaboration and shared objectives.

A business plan is a vital document that provides structure, direction, and a strategic roadmap for a new business. It helps entrepreneurs clarify their objectives, make informed decisions, secure financing, and navigate challenges. It includes key sections such as the Executive Summary (most important), Team information (next most), Product or Service (simplified), Landscape & Opportunity, SWOT analysis and Financials.

THIS IS A SAMPLE MINI BUSINESS PLAN AND PITCH DECK FOR A GIFT HAMPER COMPANY CALLED GIFT HAVEN

EXECUTIVE SUMMARY:

Gift Haven is an online company specializing in the sale of beautifully curated gift hampers. Our mission is to provide unique and personalized gifting solutions that create lasting impressions. With a focus on high-quality products, exceptional customer service, and a user-friendly online platform, Gift Haven aims to become a leading player in the online gift industry.

We are seeking to raise $200,000 in funding to support our growth and expansion plans. The investment will be utilized for the following key areas:

1. Inventory Expansion: A significant portion of the funding will be allocated towards expanding our inventory of high-

quality products sourced from local artisans and vendors. This will enable us to offer a wider selection of gift options, catering to a diverse range of customer preferences and occasions.

2. Marketing and Branding: We will allocate funds towards marketing and branding initiatives to increase our brand awareness and reach our target audience. This includes digital marketing campaigns, social media advertising, influencer collaborations, and search engine optimization to drive website traffic and boost sales.

3. Technology and Infrastructure: We will invest in upgrading our website infrastructure, enhancing the user experience, and improving the efficiency of our online platform. This will include implementing advanced e-commerce features, optimizing mobile responsiveness, and ensuring secure payment processing.

4. Operational Expansion: The funds will support the expansion of our operations, including hiring additional staff members to handle order fulfilment, customer service, and logistics. We will also invest in streamlining our supply chain management and improving inventory management systems.

5. Research and Development: We believe in continuous innovation and staying ahead of market trends. A portion of the funding will be allocated to research and development efforts, allowing us to introduce new product lines, improve customization options, and enhance the overall gifting experience for our customers.

Our financial projections demonstrate strong growth potential and a clear path to profitability. With the infusion of funds, we anticipate accelerated revenue growth, increased market penetration, and enhanced operational capabilities.

We invite investors who share our vision to join us in revolutionizing the gifting industry. Together, we can leverage the growing market opportunity, create memorable gift experiences, and establish Gift Haven as the go-to destination for curated gift hampers.

 **The Executive Summary must contain all key points and simply explain the product or service. If not compelling a potential investor will often not read any further.**

FOUNDERS SUMMARY:

Gift Haven is a result of the vision, expertise, and dedication of its three founders. Each founder brings unique skills and experiences to the company, complementing one another and collectively driving its success.

1. [Founder 1 - Name]:

As the visionary behind Gift Haven, [Founder 1] has a keen understanding of the gifting industry and a passion for creating exceptional experiences. With a background in marketing and a strong creative flair, [Founder 1] is responsible for shaping the brand identity, curating the product range, and overseeing the overall strategic direction of the company. Their ability to identify market trends and anticipate customer needs ensures that Gift Haven remains at the forefront of the industry.

2. [Founder 2 - Name]:

[Founder 2] brings extensive experience in operations and logistics to Gift Haven. With a meticulous attention to detail and a commitment to efficiency, [Founder 2] ensures that the entire supply chain runs smoothly. Their expertise in sourcing high-quality products from local artisans and establishing strong vendor relationships ensures that each gift hamper is filled with premium items that delight recipients. [Founder 2]'s expertise is essential in maintaining the company's commitment to quality and timely delivery.

3. [Founder 3 - Name]:

[Founder 3] is the driving force behind Gift Haven's customer-centric approach. With a background in customer service and relationship management, [Founder 3] understands the importance of exceptional customer experiences. Their dedication to providing personalized assistance, prompt responses, and effective problem-solving ensures that every customer interaction is positive and memorable. [Founder 3]'s ability to connect with customers and build long-lasting relationships contributes to Gift Haven's reputation for outstanding service.

Together, the founders of Gift Haven combine their expertise in marketing, operations, and customer service to create a thriving online gift hamper company. Their shared commitment to quality, customization, and superior customer experiences is the foundation of the company's success. With their collective vision, strategic mindset, and passion for delivering exceptional gift solutions, the founders are poised to lead Gift Haven to become a trusted and sought-after brand in the gifting industry.

MARKET OPPORTUNITY:

Gift Haven operates in a highly promising market with significant growth potential. The gift industry has undergone a notable transformation in recent years, fuelled by the increasing preference for convenient and personalized online shopping experiences. This presents a tremendous market opportunity for Gift Haven to capture a significant share and establish itself as a leader in the online gift hamper segment.

1. Growing Demand for Online Gifting:

The shift towards online shopping has been accelerated by factors such as convenience, wider product selection, and ease of comparison. Consumers now seek unique and curated gift options that go beyond traditional offerings. Gift Haven is well-positioned to capitalize on this trend by providing a diverse range of beautifully curated gift hampers that cater to various occasions and personalization preferences.

2. Rise in Personalization and Customization:

Today's consumers value personalized experiences, and gifting is no exception. Gift Haven recognizes this trend and offers a unique opportunity for customers to create customized gift hampers tailored to their recipients' preferences. By providing a wide selection of high-quality products and flexible customization options, Gift Haven caters to the growing demand for personalized gifting experiences.

3. Increasing Occasions and Celebrations:

Celebrations and special occasions occur throughout the year, providing a continuous market for gift hampers. Birthdays, weddings, anniversaries, baby showers, holidays, and corporate events are just a few examples of occasions where gift hampers are in high demand. Gift Haven's extensive product range and ability to curate hampers for different occasions positions the company to capture a wide range of customer needs.

4. Corporate Gifting Market:

In addition to individual consumers, corporate clients represent a lucrative market segment. Gift Haven has the opportunity to tap into the corporate gifting market by offering tailored gift solutions for employee recognition programs, client appreciation, and corporate events. This segment offers the potential for bulk orders, recurring business, and long-term partnerships, contributing to revenue growth and brand visibility.

5. Emphasis on Unique and Memorable Experiences:

As consumers seek meaningful and memorable experiences, the concept of gifting has evolved beyond mere material possessions. Gift Haven's focus on beautifully curated hampers filled with high-quality products aligns with the desire to create lasting impressions and emotional connections. By providing unique and thoughtfully designed gift experiences, Gift Haven is well-positioned to meet the evolving demands of discerning consumers.

With the growing demand for personalized, curated, and convenient gift options, Gift Haven has a substantial market opportunity. By leveraging its unique product offerings, exceptional customer service, and strategic marketing efforts, Gift Haven can successfully penetrate the market, capture a significant share, and become a trusted destination for memorable gift experiences.

12 *Show that you know your market and have researched the opportunity. So many startups go headfirst into creating a product convinced there is a market for it.*

SWOT ANALYSIS

Strengths:

1. Unique and curated gift hampers: Gift Haven offers a wide range of beautifully curated gift hampers, providing customers with unique and personalized gifting options that set us apart from competitors.

2. High-quality products: We prioritize sourcing high-quality products from local artisans and vendors, ensuring that our gift hampers are filled with premium items that create a lasting impression.

3. Exceptional customer service: We are committed to providing exceptional customer service, including prompt responses to inquiries, efficient order processing, and

timely delivery, which contributes to customer satisfaction and loyalty.

4. Online presence and user-friendly website: Our online platform is user-friendly, allowing customers to easily browse, select, and customize gift hampers according to their preferences. We leverage digital marketing strategies to reach a wider audience and increase brand visibility.

Weaknesses:

1. Reliance on third-party logistics: As an online business, we depend on reliable logistics providers for timely and accurate delivery. Any disruptions or delays in the logistics chain could impact our customer experience and reputation.

2. Limited brand recognition: Being a new company, Gift Haven may initially face challenges in building brand recognition and establishing a strong presence in the highly competitive online gifting market.

Opportunities:

1. Growing online gift market: The online gifting market is experiencing significant growth, with increasing numbers of consumers opting for the convenience of online shopping. This provides a vast opportunity for Gift Haven to capture a larger market share.

2. Partnerships and collaborations: Forming strategic partnerships with complementary businesses, such as event planners, wedding venues, or corporate clients, can expand our customer base and create mutually beneficial collaborations.

3. Expansion into corporate gifting: By targeting corporate clients and offering tailored gift solutions for employee recognition programs, client appreciation, or corporate events, Gift Haven can tap into a lucrative market segment.

Threats:

1. Intense competition: The online gifting industry is highly competitive, with numerous established players and new entrants. Competing with larger and more established brands may pose a challenge in terms of market penetration and differentiation.

2. Economic downturn: Economic fluctuations and recessions can impact consumer spending on discretionary items like gift hampers. A decrease in consumer purchasing power could affect sales and revenue.

3. Changing consumer preferences and trends: It is important for Gift Haven to stay attuned to evolving consumer preferences, gifting trends, and shifts in market demand. Failure to adapt and innovate accordingly may result in losing market share to more agile competitors.

By identifying these strengths, weaknesses, opportunities, and threats, Gift Haven can develop strategies to leverage its advantages, overcome challenges, and capitalize on opportunities to achieve sustainable growth and competitive advantage in the online gift hamper market.

13   *SWOT Analysis is great for highlighting areas that need addressing*

SALES AND MARKETING STRATEGY FOR GIFT HAVEN:

1. Target Audience:

   Identify the target audience for Gift Haven's gift hampers, including both individual consumers and corporate clients. Define buyer personas based on demographics, interests, and gifting occasions to tailor marketing messages and product offerings.

2. Branding and Positioning:

   Develop a strong and memorable brand identity that reflects Gift Haven's values, unique selling proposition, and commitment to quality and customization. Position the brand as a trusted source for beautifully curated gift hampers that make a lasting impression.

3. Online Presence:

   Establish a user-friendly website that showcases the range of gift hampers and allows customers to easily browse, select, and customize their purchases. Optimize the website for search engines to increase visibility and organic traffic. Utilize high-quality product images, compelling descriptions, and customer reviews to enhance the online shopping experience.

4. Content Marketing:

   Create valuable and engaging content related to gifting, celebrations, and occasions through blog posts, articles, and social media posts. Provide useful tips, gift guides, and personalization ideas to position Gift Haven as an industry expert. Leverage storytelling and visual content to evoke emotions and resonate with the target audience.

5. Social Media Marketing:

Utilize popular social media platforms such as Facebook, Instagram, Pinterest, and Twitter to reach and engage with potential customers. Share visually appealing images, videos, and stories showcasing the range of gift hampers, customization options, and satisfied customers. Collaborate with influencers and run targeted ad campaigns to expand reach and drive website traffic.

6. Email Marketing:

Implement an email marketing strategy to nurture customer relationships and drive repeat purchases. Collect customer email addresses through website sign-ups or purchases and send personalized offers, discounts, and exclusive promotions. Use email campaigns to highlight new product launches, seasonal offers, and upcoming events.

7. Referral Program and Loyalty Rewards:

Implement a referral program to encourage satisfied customers to refer their friends and family to Gift Haven. Offer incentives such as discounts or freebies for successful referrals. Develop a loyalty program that rewards repeat customers with exclusive perks, early access to new products, or special discounts.

8. Collaborations and Partnerships:

Form strategic partnerships with complementary businesses, such as event planners, wedding venues, or corporate clients. Offer exclusive discounts or customized gift solutions for their clients or employees. Collaborate with influencers, bloggers, and local businesses to cross-promote products and increase brand awareness.

9. Customer Experience and Reviews:

Prioritize exceptional customer service to ensure a positive shopping experience. Provide prompt responses to inquiries, offer personalized recommendations, and resolve any issues efficiently. Encourage customers to leave reviews and testimonials to build social proof and trust.

10. Analytics and Measurement:

Regularly analyse key performance indicators (KPIs) such as website traffic, conversion rates, customer acquisition costs, and customer lifetime value. Use analytics tools to track the effectiveness of marketing campaigns and adjust strategies accordingly. Continuously refine and optimize marketing efforts based on data-driven insights.

By implementing this sales and marketing strategy, Gift Haven can effectively reach its target audience, build brand awareness, and drive sales. It is important to monitor results, adapt to changing market dynamics, and stay updated with emerging marketing trends to maintain a competitive edge.

FINANCIAL PROJECTIONS

YEAR 1

Sales Forecast:

- Quarter 1	50000
- Quarter 2	60000
- Quarter 3	70000
- Quarter 4	<u>80000</u>
Year 1 Total	**260000**

Cost of Goods Sold (COGS):	**130000**

(Assuming a 50% COGS margin)

Operating Expenses

- Marketing and Advertising	30000
- Website Maintenance and Hosting	10000
- Administrative Expenses	20000
- Salaries and Wages	<u>50000</u>
Total	**110000**

Profit Before Tax	**20000**

(Sales - COGS - Operating Expenses)

Net Profit	15000

(Assuming a tax rate of 25%)

YEAR 2

Sales Forecast:

- Quarter 1	80000
- Quarter 2	90000
- Quarter 3	100000
- Quarter 4	<u>110000</u>
Year 2 Total	**380000**

Cost of Goods Sold (COGS):	190000
(Assuming a 50% COGS margin)	

Operating Expenses

- Marketing and Advertising	35000
- Website Maintenance and Hosting	12000
- Administrative Expenses	25000
- Salaries and Wages	<u>55000</u>
Total	**127000**

Profit Before Tax	**63000**
(Sales - COGS - Operating Expenses)	

Net Profit	47250
(Assuming a tax rate of 25%)	

YEAR 3

Sales Forecast:

- Quarter 1	100000
- Quarter 2	120000
- Quarter 3	140000
- Quarter 4	160000
Year 3 Total	**520000**

Cost of Goods Sold (COGS):	260000
(Assuming a 50% COGS margin)	

Operating Expenses

- Marketing and Advertising	40000
- Website Maintenance and Hosting	14000
- Administrative Expenses	30000
- Salaries and Wages	60000
Total	**144000**

Profit Before Tax	**116000**
(Sales - COGS - Operating Expenses)	

Net Profit	87000
(Assuming a tax rate of 25%)	

14   *KNOW YOUR NUMBERS*

THE PITCH DECK

The pitch deck is basically a simplfied graphical interpretation of your business plan. A well-designed pitch deck is a powerful tool for entrepreneurs seeking investment for their business. It is a visual presentation that conveys the key aspects of a business, highlighting its value proposition, market opportunity, and financial projections. Here are the key reasons why a well-designed pitch deck is crucial when looking for investment:

1. Captures Investor Attention: Investors are often presented with numerous investment opportunities, and their time is limited. A well-designed pitch deck grabs their attention from the start and quickly communicates the unique aspects of the business. Visual elements, compelling graphics, and a clear structure make the pitch deck visually appealing and engaging, increasing the chances of capturing the investor's interest.

2. Conveys the Value Proposition: A pitch deck succinctly communicates the value proposition of the business, highlighting its unique selling points, competitive advantage, and market differentiators. It explains why the business stands out in the market and why investors should consider it as a promising investment opportunity. A well-crafted pitch deck clearly articulates the business's value proposition, compelling investors to learn more.

3. Tells a Compelling Story: Humans are wired to respond to stories. A well-designed pitch deck helps entrepreneurs weave a compelling narrative that connects with investors on an emotional level. By presenting the problem the business solves, the market opportunity, and the vision for

the future, a pitch deck creates a story that investors can relate to and become invested in. This emotional connection can significantly influence investment decisions.

4. Provides Structure and Focus: A pitch deck forces entrepreneurs to distil their business idea into its most essential components. It provides a structure that guides the presentation, ensuring that key information is communicated effectively. By focusing on the most critical aspects of the business, a well-designed pitch deck avoids overwhelming investors with unnecessary details and allows them to grasp the key elements quickly.

5. Demonstrates Market Opportunity: A pitch deck showcases the market opportunity for the business, including market size, growth potential, and target audience. It presents market research, competitor analysis, and customer insights to demonstrate the viability and potential of the business. By clearly articulating the market opportunity, a pitch deck provides investors with the necessary information to evaluate the business's scalability and revenue potential.

6. Illustrates Financial Projections: Investors want to understand the financial potential of the business. A well-designed pitch deck presents financial projections, including revenue forecasts, profitability, and return on investment. It provides a clear picture of the business's financial performance and growth trajectory, enabling investors to assess the potential for a profitable investment.

7. Enhances Credibility and Professionalism: A professionally designed pitch deck demonstrates the entrepreneur's commitment, attention to detail, and professionalism. It shows that the entrepreneur has put in the effort to craft

a persuasive and visually appealing presentation. A well-designed pitch deck reflects positively on the entrepreneur and the business, enhancing credibility and increasing the chances of attracting investment.

8. Facilitates Communication and Discussion: The pitch deck serves as a communication tool during investor meetings and presentations. It provides a structure for the entrepreneur to deliver a concise and impactful pitch, setting the stage for further discussion and due diligence. A well-designed pitch deck facilitates a smooth flow of information and promotes meaningful dialogue between the entrepreneur and the investors.

15	*Keep your Pitch Deck no more than 15 Slides*

CONSIDERATIONS

Ideally 10 – 15 slides and be light on text.

Invest some $ on design or try templates on platforms such as Canva. Design is hugely important, and the deck is also a reflection of your business so put best foot forward.

You may have different slides depending on your business/industry.

The Pitch Deck is largely pulled from key areas of a business plan.

Practice, Practice, Practice

16	*Keep you Deck light on text and use engaging imagery*

OUTLINE FOR A 10-SLIDE PITCH DECK FOR GIFT HAVEN:

Slide 1: Company Logo and Name
- Display the Gift Haven logo and company name to establish brand identity.

Slide 2: Problem Statement
- Highlight the challenges and pain points faced by consumers when it comes to finding unique and personalized gift options.

Slide 3: Solution
- Explain how Gift Haven addresses the problem by offering beautifully curated gift hampers that can be customized to suit individual preferences and occasions.

Slide 4: Market Opportunity
- Present market research and statistics showcasing the growth and potential of the online gifting industry, emphasizing the demand for personalized and convenient gifting solutions.

Slide 5: Competitive Advantage
- Highlight the unique selling points that set Gift Haven apart from competitors, such as our focus on high-quality products, extensive customization options, and exceptional customer service.

Slide 6: Business Model

- Explain the revenue streams, pricing strategy, and target customer segments, including both individual consumers and corporate clients.

Slide 7: Marketing and Sales Strategy

- Describe the sales and marketing approach, including digital marketing initiatives, social media campaigns, influencer collaborations, and partnerships with event planners and corporate clients.

Slide 8: Financial Projections

- Showcase the projected financial growth and profitability of Gift Haven based on market analysis and revenue forecasts, demonstrating the return on investment for potential investors.

Slide 9: Team

- Introduce the founders and key team members, highlighting their expertise and experience in the gifting industry, marketing, operations, and customer service.

Slide 10: Funding Request and Use of Funds

- Clearly state the amount of funding sought and how it will be utilized to support inventory expansion, marketing efforts, technology upgrades, operational expansion, and research and development.

Remember to keep the slides visually appealing with clear and concise content. Utilize graphics, images, and charts wherever possible to enhance the presentation.

17 — When it comes to presenting your business – PRACTICE, PRACTICE, PRACTICE

CHAPTER

3

STARTING OUT

IN THIS CHAPTER WE'RE going to look at the research and analysis stage. This is hugely important. From the outset, you need to make sure that you have your business model right. What is it that you're looking to do? Are you looking to grow a business that has residual income? If so you need to make sure that the annual fee or the monthly fee, whatever it is you're looking to charge is achievable. If you're looking at selling a product or a service, you need to make sure that your gross margins are achievable. So again, at this stage it's important to get out, talk to potential users or prospective customers and get their feedback. Obviously you don't have a product at this stage, but it is important from the get-go to make sure that the model of business you are looking to set up is doable.

Each business type will have some sort of criteria which need to be met, to make that business viable. So again, at this stage research is really, really important. There's rarely enough done at the analysis stage. When starting a business, founders will have different business considerations depending on the sector or industry they are operating in. Let's look at a few;

BRAND AND LOGO

It is crucial to consider your brand and logo. The brand and logo serve as the face of your business, representing its identity and values. They play a significant role in attracting customers, building trust, and differentiating your business from competitors. Here are four reasons why it is important to prioritize your brand and logo when launching a business.

First impressions matter, and your brand and logo are often the first elements that potential customers encounter. A well-designed logo creates an immediate visual impact and communicates professionalism and credibility. It conveys a sense of quality and expertise, which can help establish trust with your target audience. A poorly designed or generic logo, on the other hand, may give the impression of a lack of attention to detail or a subpar offering. By investing in a well-crafted logo, you can make a positive and memorable first impression, increasing the chances of attracting and retaining customers.

Your brand and logo play a vital role in distinguishing your business from competitors. In today's crowded marketplace, having a unique and recognizable brand identity is crucial for standing out. A distinctive logo helps your business become instantly recognizable and memorable. It allows customers to differentiate your products or services from others and develop a sense of loyalty. Additionally, a well-defined brand identity that is consistent across all touchpoints—such as your website, packaging, marketing materials, and social media—creates a cohesive and professional image, enhancing brand recognition and recall.

Design - When it comes to designing your brand, consider getting a quality designer. There are many marketplaces for graphic designers such as Peopleperhour, Fiver.com etc. I would recommend spending some budget on a good designer when it comes to getting a logo created. It doesnt have to be more than $100 but it's like everything else in life, you get what you pay for. It's most definitely worth going the extra mile to get a great logo designed and something that's transferable across various media. It must work in print, online, video etc. So, again, a really well rated designer is more likely to deliver a great quality logo for you, but you might end up paying a little bit more. But it's an investment that's worthwhile.

A strong brand and logo can evoke emotions and connect with your target audience on a deeper level. By carefully crafting your brand identity, you can align it with your target customers' values, aspirations, and desires. A thoughtfully designed logo can evoke specific emotions, whether it's trust, excitement, or sophistication, and create a positive perception of your business. When customers feel an emotional connection with your brand, they are more likely to engage with it, become repeat customers, and advocate for your business through word-of-mouth referrals.

As your business grows, your brand and logo become valuable assets. They become synonymous with your business's reputation and can influence its success in the long term. A strong brand with a well-established logo can command higher prices, attract better partnerships, and increase customer loyalty. Moreover, a recognizable brand can provide a competitive advantage and open doors to new opportunities, such as collaborations, sponsorships, or licensing agreements. By investing in your brand and logo early on, you set the foundation for future growth and expansion.

In conclusion, giving careful consideration to your brand and logo is essential when starting a business. They shape the perception of your business, differentiate it from competitors, create emotional connections with customers, and become valuable assets over time. By investing in a well-crafted brand and logo, you establish a strong foundation for your business's success, increase its visibility, and foster customer loyalty. Remember, your brand and logo are not just visual elements; they represent the values, personality, and aspirations of your business, making them critical components of your overall strategy.

<table>
<tr><td>18</td><td>Invest some $ in getting a good logo and branding for your business</td></tr>
</table>

BE CLEAR ON YOUR BUSINESS MODEL

There are various types of business models that exist across different industries and sectors. These models define how a business generates revenue, serves customers, and operates within the marketplace. Let's explore some of the most common business models, ranging from those centered around annual recurring revenues to traditional high street retail.

1. Annual Recurring Revenue (ARR) Model:

This model focuses on generating predictable, recurring revenue streams. It typically involves providing products or services through subscriptions or memberships. Examples include software-as-a-service (SaaS) companies that charge customers a monthly or annual fee for using their platforms, or membership-based businesses that offer exclusive benefits and access for a recurring fee. ARR models benefit from a stable customer base and can generate consistent revenue over time.

2. E-commerce and Online Retail Model:

In recent years, the e-commerce model has experienced significant growth. It involves selling products or services online, leveraging digital platforms and technologies. E-commerce businesses can operate through their own websites or online marketplaces, facilitating transactions and providing a seamless shopping experience. This model offers convenience, a global reach, and the potential for scalability.

3. Marketplace Model:

Marketplace models bring together buyers and sellers in a virtual environment. The marketplace acts as a platform where multiple vendors can list their products or services, connecting them with potential customers. Examples include platforms like Amazon, eBay, and Airbnb. These models derive revenue through transaction fees, commissions, or advertising.

4. Franchise Model:

The franchise model allows entrepreneurs to replicate a proven business concept and brand by purchasing the rights to operate under an established franchise. Franchisees benefit from a recognized brand, operational support, and marketing assistance. In return, they pay fees or royalties to the franchisor. This model enables both parties to grow their businesses and expand into new markets.

5. Brick-and-Mortar Retail Model:

The traditional high street retail model involves operating physical stores where customers can browse, try on, and purchase products. These businesses typically have a local or regional customer base. The success of brick-and-mortar retailers often depends on factors such as location, foot traffic, and customer experience. In recent years, many high street retailers have integrated e-commerce into their operations to complement their physical stores.

6. Subscription Model:

The subscription model offers customers access to products or services on a recurring basis. This could involve subscriptions for media streaming services (e.g., Netflix), subscription boxes (e.g., Birchbox), or curated product bundles (e.g., Dollar Shave Club). By charging customers a regular fee, businesses can maintain ongoing relationships and provide a steady revenue stream.

7. Freemium Model:

The freemium model combines free and premium offerings. Businesses provide a basic version of their product or service for free, enticing users to upgrade to a paid premium version with additional features or enhanced functionality. This model is commonly seen in software, mobile apps, and online platforms, aiming to attract a large user base and convert a portion of them into paying customers.

8. Peer-to-Peer (P2P) Model:

P2P models enable individuals to engage in direct transactions with one another without intermediaries. Popular examples include ride-sharing platforms like Uber and home-sharing platforms like Airbnb. These models provide a platform for people to offer their services or assets to others, often earning a commission or transaction fee.

These are just a few examples of the diverse business models that exist today. Each model has its own advantages, challenges, and revenue-generation strategies. The choice of a business model depends on factors such as the industry, target market, competitive landscape, and the unique value proposition of the business. By understanding and selecting an appropriate business model, entrepreneurs can set the foundation for success and adapt to the changing needs of their customers and market.

19	*Understand your business model. This will be needed also for valuation.*

WEBSITE SOFTWARE

As pretty much every business will require a website, we will look at some of the Pros and Cons of some of the leading platforms. Website platforms play a crucial role in establishing and managing an online presence. Two popular website platforms are WordPress and Wix, each offering distinct advantages and disadvantages. Here we will explore the pros and cons of these platforms to help you make an informed decision for your website needs.

WordPress:

WordPress is a versatile and widely used content management system (CMS) that powers over 40% of all websites on the internet. Here are the pros and cons of using WordPress:

Pros:

1. Flexibility: WordPress offers unmatched flexibility, allowing you to create any type of website, from simple blogs to complex e-commerce sites. Its extensive library of themes and plugins enables you to customize your website to meet your specific requirements.

2. Open-source: WordPress is an open-source platform, meaning it is constantly improved and updated by a large community of developers. This results in frequent security patches, bug fixes, and new features, ensuring your website remains up to date.

3. SEO-friendly: WordPress provides excellent search engine optimization (SEO) capabilities, including customizable permalinks, meta tags, and SEO plugins. This helps improve your website's visibility in search engine rankings, driving more organic traffic.

4. Community and support: WordPress has a vast community of users and developers who actively contribute to forums, support groups, and online resources. Finding assistance, tutorials, and guidance is relatively easy due to the platform's popularity.

20 *Try and generate a recurring revenue from your customer. You have done the hard work in getting the sale and customers are usually happy to pay 10%-20% of the sale cost annually for some sort of support, service or just comfort. This can be a great profit generator for a business but MAKE SURE that it is provided at a low cost (ideally 70%+ gross margin)*

21 *Get a good website developed and don't cut corners. It is often the only impression a potential customer has of your business.*

Cons:

1. Learning curve: Despite its user-friendly interface, WordPress has a steeper learning curve compared to simpler website builders. Beginners may require some time to familiarize themselves with the platform and its features.

2. Self-hosting: To use WordPress, you need to set up your own web hosting, domain name, and handle software updates. This level of control may be overwhelming for users who prefer an all-in-one solution.

3. Security vulnerabilities: Due to its popularity, WordPress can be a target for hackers. While regular updates help mitigate security risks, users must remain vigilant and implement additional security measures, such as using strong passwords and security plugins.

Wix:

Wix is a popular website builder that simplifies the website creation process through its drag-and-drop interface. Let's explore the pros and cons of using Wix:

Pros:

1. Ease of use: Wix is known for its user-friendly interface, making it ideal for beginners with little to no technical skills. Its drag-and-drop editor allows users to build websites quickly without any coding knowledge.

2. All-in-one solution: Wix provides web hosting, domain registration, and security features in one package. This simplifies the setup process as everything is managed within the platform.

3. Design options: Wix offers a wide range of visually appealing templates that cater to various industries and website types. Customization is intuitive, allowing users to modify templates to suit their brand aesthetics.

4. Customer support: Wix provides comprehensive customer support through various channels, including phone, email, and live chat. This ensures that users can receive assistance promptly when facing issues or needing guidance.

Cons:

1. Limited flexibility: While Wix's drag-and-drop editor is easy to use, it also restricts the level of customization compared to WordPress. Users may encounter limitations when trying to implement specific design or functionality requirements.

2. Template dependency: Once you choose a template in Wix, switching to a different one can be challenging. This can become problematic if you want to redesign your website or migrate to another platform in the future.

3. Cost: While Wix offers free plans, they come with limitations and Wix branding. To access advanced features, remove ads, and use a custom domain, users need to upgrade to premium plans, which can be more expensive than self-hosted WordPress.

22   *Get the best domain name you can for your business.*

23   *Get objective feedback where you can at all stages*

OTHER SOFTWARE NEEDS

Starting a business in today's digital landscape requires leveraging various types of software to streamline operations, enhance productivity, and drive growth. From communication and project management to finance and marketing, software solutions play a crucial role in supporting different aspects of a business. Here, we will explore some of the essential software types you may need when starting a business.

1. Communication and Collaboration Tools:

Efficient communication is vital for any business. Email clients like Microsoft Outlook or Gmail enable you to manage professional correspondence, while instant messaging platforms like Slack or Microsoft Teams facilitate real-time communication among team members. Video conferencing software such as Zoom or Microsoft Teams can help you conduct virtual meetings and connect with clients or remote team members. Collaboration tools like Google Workspace or Microsoft 365 provide shared document editing, file storage, and project management capabilities to foster teamwork.

2. Project Management Software:

When launching a business, organizing tasks and managing projects is crucial. Project management tools like Trello, Asana, or Jira help you create and assign tasks, track progress, set deadlines, and collaborate with team members. These platforms provide a centralized workspace where you can visualize project timelines, allocate resources, and ensure timely completion of tasks.

3. Customer Relationship Management (CRM) Software:

Maintaining strong relationships with customers is key to business success. CRM software, such as Salesforce, HubSpot, or Zoho CRM, helps you manage customer interactions, track sales opportunities, and analyse customer data. With a CRM system, you can store customer information, track communication history, automate sales processes, and gain insights to enhance customer satisfaction and drive sales growth.

4. Accounting and Financial Software:

Proper financial management is critical for any business. Accounting software like QuickBooks, Xero, or FreshBooks allows you to track income and expenses, generate invoices, manage payroll, and monitor financial statements. These tools provide a comprehensive view of your business's financial health, enabling you to make informed decisions and ensure compliance with accounting regulations.

5. Human Resources (HR) Management Software:

As your business grows, managing human resources becomes increasingly important. HR software solutions like BambooHR, Gusto, or Zenefits assist in various HR functions, including employee onboarding, time tracking, leave management, performance evaluations, and benefits administration. These tools streamline HR processes, enhance employee engagement, and ensure compliance with HR policies and regulations.

6. E-commerce Platforms:

If you plan to sell products or services online, an e-commerce platform is essential. Platforms like Shopify, WooCommerce (a WordPress plugin), or BigCommerce provide user-friendly interfaces to set up and manage online stores. They offer features for product catalogue management, secure payment processing, inventory tracking, order fulfilment, and customer support, helping you establish and grow your online presence.

7. Marketing and Social Media Management Tools:

Promoting your business and reaching your target audience requires effective marketing strategies. Software tools like Mailchimp, Hootsuite, or Buffer can assist in email marketing, social media management, and content scheduling. These platforms allow you to automate marketing campaigns, manage social media accounts, analyse engagement metrics, and build a strong online presence.

8. Analytics and Data Visualization Tools:

Understanding data and making data-driven decisions is crucial for business growth. Analytics tools like Google Analytics, Tableau, or Power BI enable you to collect and analyse data related to website traffic, customer behaviour, and marketing campaigns. These tools provide insights through visualizations, dashboards, and reports, helping you optimize your business strategies and improve performance.

9. Cybersecurity and Data Protection Software:

Protecting your business's sensitive data and ensuring cybersecurity is essential. Antivirus software, firewalls, and virtual private networks (VPNs) help safeguard your business from malware, data breaches, and cyber threats. Tools like LastPass or Dashlane can assist in managing strong.

24 ***Identify the software that your business needs***

SOCIAL MEDIA

At the outset, you will want to think about the social media needs of your business. It's getting more and more competitive to sell via social media. And the likes of Facebook now require you spending a huge amount of money to promote your business, even to your own Facebook followers.

In today's digital age, social media has become an integral part of marketing strategies for businesses, including start-ups. Social media platforms offer a wide range of opportunities to engage with potential customers, build brand awareness, and drive business growth. Let's explore some of the social media platforms that you might want to use to establish a strong online presence.

Facebook:

With over 2.8 billion monthly active users, Facebook is the largest social media platform. It provides businesses with extensive opportunities to target specific audiences through demographic and interest-based advertising. Facebook Pages allow start-ups to create a branded presence, share updates, engage with customers, and collect valuable feedback. Additionally, Facebook groups can be utilized to build a community around your brand, fostering discussions and loyalty.

Instagram:

Focused on visual content, Instagram boasts more than 1 billion users. It is particularly beneficial for start-ups in visually driven industries such as fashion, food, and travel. By sharing high-quality photos and videos, businesses can showcase their products, tell their brand story, and interact with their target audience. Instagram also offers features like Instagram Stories and IGTV, providing additional avenues for engaging and entertaining content.

Twitter:

Twitter is a real-time, fast-paced platform that allows businesses to share short, concise messages known as tweets. It is ideal for start-ups looking to engage in conversations, share industry insights, and provide customer support. The use of hashtags makes it easy to join trending discussions and reach a broader audience. Twitter is also a valuable platform for networking and building relationships with industry influencers and thought leaders.

LinkedIn:

LinkedIn is a professional networking platform with over 740 million users. It is highly beneficial for B2B start-ups and those targeting professionals in specific industries. Businesses can create a company page to share updates, job postings, and thought leadership content. LinkedIn groups provide opportunities for engaging with industry peers, participating in discussions, and establishing expertise. Additionally, LinkedIn advertising offers precise targeting options to reach relevant professionals.

YouTube:

YouTube is the second-largest search engine after Google, making it an excellent platform for start-ups to create and share video content. It allows businesses to showcase products, provide tutorials, share testimonials, and demonstrate expertise. YouTube also enables monetization through ads and sponsorships, offering potential revenue streams. Integrating YouTube videos into other social media channels can increase reach and engagement.

Pinterest:

Pinterest is a visual discovery platform that allows users to find and save ideas on various topics. It is particularly useful for start-ups in industries like fashion, interior design, food, and crafts. By creating visually appealing pins, businesses can drive traffic to their websites and e-commerce platforms. Pinterest also offers advertising options, making it easier to reach users who are actively seeking inspiration and ideas.

TikTok:

TikTok has rapidly gained popularity, especially among younger audiences. This short-form video platform provides a unique opportunity for start-ups to create entertaining and engaging content that resonates with their target market. TikTok's algorithm driven "For You" page can help content go viral, increasing brand visibility. Influencer collaborations and hashtag challenges can also amplify reach and engagement.

Snapchat:

Snapchat is a multimedia messaging app that allows users to share photos and videos that disappear after a short period. It appeals to a younger demographic and is ideal for start-ups targeting Gen Z and millennials. Snapchat's features like filters, lenses, and geofilters enable businesses to create interactive and playful content. Sponsored lenses and ads can further boost brand visibility.

Reddit:

Reddit is a platform consisting of various communities called "subreddits." It is known for its active and engaged user base. Start-ups can participate in relevant subreddits to share knowledge, answer questions, and build credibility.

 **Identify the social media channels that are right for your business. You may only need 1 or 2.**

DEVELOP A CONTENT STRATEGY

Most companies will engage with their customers through content generation with newsletters, blogs and the like and if you are working on social media, paid advertising with a good content strategy, can position your business as experts in you sector and be great for helping to drive sales.

Developing a content strategy is a critical step in growing organic leads for your business. A well-planned content strategy helps you attract, engage, and convert your target audience into loyal customers. In this article, we will explore the key steps to developing an effective content strategy that drives organic lead generation.

1. Define Your Target Audience:

The first step in developing a content strategy is understanding your target audience. Identify their demographics, interests, pain points, and motivations. This information will shape the type of content you create and the channels you use to reach them. Conduct market research, analyse customer data, and gather feedback to gain insights into your audience's preferences and needs.

2. Set Clear Goals:

Establish clear and measurable goals for your content strategy. Are you aiming to increase brand awareness, generate leads, drive website traffic, or promote specific products/services? Setting SMART goals (specific, measurable, achievable, relevant, and time-bound) ensures your content strategy aligns with your overall business objectives.

3. Conduct Keyword Research:

Keyword research is essential for optimizing your content for search engines. Identify relevant keywords and phrases that your target audience is likely to use when searching for solutions or information related to your business. Tools like Google Keyword Planner, SEMrush, or Moz Keyword Explorer can help you identify high-volume and low-competition keywords.

4. Create a Content Calendar:

Develop a content calendar to organize your content creation and distribution schedule. Plan your content topics, formats, and distribution channels in advance. A content calendar ensures consistent output, helps you align content with seasonal trends or campaigns, and maintains a steady flow of engaging content to attract and retain your audience.

26

Make sure your content is scheduled and regular. A good post a week is often enough.

5. Diversify Content Formats:

Different people consume content in different ways. Diversify your content formats to cater to varying preferences. Consider creating blog posts, videos, infographics, podcasts, case studies, whitepapers, webinars, and social media posts. Experiment with different formats to see what resonates most with your audience and adjust your strategy accordingly.

6. Develop High-Quality Content:

Focus on creating high-quality, valuable content that addresses your audience's pain points and provides solutions. Research industry trends, conduct surveys, and leverage your expertise to develop content that positions your business as a trusted authority. Engage your audience through storytelling, actionable tips, expert interviews, and relevant examples.

7. Optimize for SEO:

Optimize your content for search engines to increase visibility and organic traffic. Incorporate target keywords naturally throughout your content, including headings, subheadings, meta tags, and image alt tags. Ensure your website has a clean URL structure, fast loading times, and mobile responsiveness. Internal linking and backlinking to authoritative sources also improve SEO.

8. Promote Your Content:

Creating great content is not enough; you need to promote it effectively. Share your content on relevant social media platforms, email newsletters, industry forums, and online communities. Engage with your audience through comments, shares, and discussions. Collaborate with influencers or industry partners to amplify your reach. Guest posting on reputable websites can also drive traffic and establish your expertise.

9. Capture and Nurture Leads:

Include lead capture forms or call-to-action (CTA) buttons strategically within your content. Offer valuable content upgrades such as e-books, templates, or exclusive access in exchange for contact information. Use marketing automation tools to nurture leads through personalized email sequences, drip campaigns, and targeted content based on their interests and engagement levels.

10. Analyse and Optimize:

Regularly track and analyse your content performance using analytics tools like Google Analytics, social media insights, and email marketing metrics. Identify high-performing content, conversion rates, traffic sources, and user behaviour. Use this data to refine your content strategy, identify gaps, and optimize underperforming areas. Continuously test.

27   *Content is a great way of positioning your business as 'experts' within your industry*

FOCUS GROUPS

A focus group is a qualitative research method that involves bringing together a small group of individuals to gather their opinions, perceptions, and feedback on a specific topic or product. It typically involves a facilitator who guides the discussion and encourages participants to share their thoughts and experiences.

Over the years I have found these to be invaluable. They can be organised for little to no cost and are useful for so many reasons:

1. Market Research: Focus groups provide valuable insights into consumer preferences, behaviours, and needs. By gathering feedback directly from potential customers, you can better understand their motivations, pain points, and desires. This information helps you tailor your products, services, and marketing strategies to meet customer demands effectively.

2. Product Development: When launching a new product or service, focus groups can offer crucial feedback during the development phase. Participants can provide insights on product features, functionality, design, packaging, and pricing. This feedback allows you to refine and enhance your offerings to ensure they align with customer expectations.

3. Concept Testing: Focus groups are helpful for testing new business ideas or concepts before investing significant resources. By presenting your ideas to a diverse group, you can gauge their initial reactions, gather suggestions, and identify potential challenges or concerns. This feedback

enables you to make informed decisions and iterate on your concepts early on, saving time and resources in the long run.

4. Branding and Marketing: Focus groups can be instrumental in shaping your brand identity and marketing strategies. Participants' opinions on brand messaging, logos, taglines, and advertising campaigns can help you refine your brand image and ensure it resonates with your target audience. Additionally, focus groups can provide insights into the most effective marketing channels and tactics to reach and engage potential customers.

5. Customer Experience and Satisfaction: Understanding customer perceptions and experiences is vital for creating a positive customer journey. Focus groups allow you to explore customer expectations, identify pain points, and uncover areas for improvement in your products or services. This knowledge helps you enhance customer satisfaction, loyalty, and retention, which are crucial for long-term business success.

28 *Utilise your customer base with Focus Groups and get them to help you identify failings and improve your product or service*

6. Competitive Analysis: Focus groups can provide insights into customers' experiences with your competitors. By comparing your offerings to those of competitors, you can identify gaps in the market and areas where you can differentiate and provide a unique value proposition. Understanding customer perceptions of competitors'

strengths and weaknesses helps you position your business effectively.

7. Early Adopter Feedback: In the early stages of setting up a business, focus groups can help you identify potential early adopters or brand advocates. These individuals are enthusiastic about new products or concepts and can provide valuable feedback, referrals, and word-of-mouth marketing. Engaging early adopters through focus groups can help generate buzz and create a loyal customer base from the outset.

8. LAST BUT NOT LEAST Focus groups are super low cost and easy to manage. Inviter 20 or 30 customer out for some free drinks and finger food in a bar after work. Have questionnaires ready for them to fill out and let them engage with your brand. They will not only help you identify ways to improve your business but will also be key marketeers and evangelists for you.

It's important to note that focus groups have limitations. The sample size is small, and opinions may not necessarily represent the broader target market. Additionally, participants' responses can be influenced by group dynamics or individual biases. Therefore, focus groups should be used in conjunction with other research methods, such as surveys and interviews, to gain a comprehensive understanding of your market and customer base.

 **29** *Have a customer competition. Twenty winners get to go for some free drinks and participate in a focus group.*

CHAPTER
4

SALES

THE SAUSAGE FACTORY – Ideally when it comes to sales you should be looking to set up as they say, a sausage factory - where you're just knocking out your product or service as quickly and cheaply as possible with the highest gross margin. So, the objective should be to be driving down the cost of sales, increasing your profits. With a product that's focused, clear, easy to understand, provides value to the consumer and has a specific demographic to sell to.

30   *Build a sausage factory!*

THE MOST IMPORTANT ROLE IN THE COMPANY

The Head of Sales. A critical role in any company for several reasons:

1. Revenue Generation: The primary responsibility of the head of sales is to drive revenue and achieve sales targets. They are responsible for developing and implementing effective sales strategies, identifying new opportunities, and closing deals. The revenue generated through sales is the lifeblood of any business, and the head of sales plays a vital role in ensuring the financial success and growth of the company.

2. Customer Acquisition: Sales is directly involved in acquiring new customers for the company. The head of sales oversees the process of identifying potential customers, nurturing

leads, and converting them into paying clients. By effectively targeting and acquiring new customers, the head of sales expands the customer base, increases market share, and contributes to the overall growth of the company.

31 Understand your CPA (Cost per Acquisition)

3. Market Insights and Customer Feedback: The head of sales interacts directly with customers, providing them with insights into their needs, preferences, and feedback. This feedback is valuable for product development, improving customer experience, and identifying areas for innovation. The head of sales acts as a bridge between the customer and the company, ensuring that customer insights are integrated into the business strategy.

4. Relationship Management: Building strong relationships with customers is crucial for long-term success. The head of sales oversees the relationship-building process, ensuring that customers receive excellent service, address their concerns, and maintain ongoing engagement. Strong customer relationships lead to customer loyalty, repeat business, and positive referrals, all of which are vital for the company's reputation and growth.

5. Collaboration with other Departments: The head of sales collaborates closely with other departments within the company, such as marketing, product development, and customer service. They provide valuable insights into customer needs, market trends, and competitive intelligence, which help shape marketing campaigns,

product improvements, and overall business strategies. The head of sales acts as a liaison between sales and other departments, fostering cross-functional collaboration and alignment.

6. Leadership and Team Management: The head of sales is responsible for leading and managing the sales team. They recruit, train, and motivate sales professionals, setting clear goals and targets, and providing guidance and support. Effective leadership from the head of sales ensures that the sales team is motivated, productive, and equipped with the necessary skills and resources to succeed.

7. Market Intelligence and Competitive Analysis: The head of sales constantly monitors the market, competitors, and industry trends. They gather market intelligence, identify emerging opportunities, and analyse the competitive landscape. This information is crucial for making informed business decisions, staying ahead of competitors, and adapting strategies to meet changing market dynamics.

While the head of sales is a pivotal role, it's important to recognize that the success of a company depends on the collective effort of all departments and team members working together towards common goals. Each role contributes to the overall success and growth of the organization.

KNOW THESE

CPA (COST PER ACQUISITION) AND CONVERSION RATES

Cost Per Acquisition (CPA) and conversion rates are two important metrics in sales and marketing that provide insights into the effectiveness and efficiency of customer acquisition efforts. Let's explore each of these metrics in more detail:

COST PER ACQUISITION (CPA):

Cost Per Acquisition refers to the average cost incurred by a company to acquire a new customer. It is calculated by dividing the total cost of marketing and sales activities by the number of customers acquired within a specific time period.

CPA helps businesses evaluate the profitability of their marketing and sales campaigns. By comparing the CPA to the average customer lifetime value (CLV), companies can assess whether their customer acquisition efforts are generating a positive return on investment. A lower CPA indicates a more cost-effective acquisition strategy, while a higher CPA may indicate the need for optimization or adjustment of marketing tactics.

To reduce CPA, businesses can focus on targeted marketing, optimize conversion rates, and improve customer retention. By analysing the CPA for different channels, campaigns, or customer segments, companies can allocate resources effectively and prioritize investments in channels that deliver a lower CPA.

CONVERSION RATES:

Conversion rates measure the percentage of potential customers who take a desired action, such as making a purchase, signing up for a newsletter, or filling out a form. It is a key performance indicator that helps evaluate the effectiveness of a sales or marketing funnel.

High conversion rates indicate that a significant portion of the target audience is successfully moving through the conversion funnel and taking the desired action. Low conversion rates may indicate issues or barriers in the customer journey that need to be addressed.

By analysing conversion rates at different stages of the funnel, businesses can identify bottlenecks or areas for improvement. They can optimize landing pages, streamline the checkout process, improve call-to-action messaging, or enhance customer support to increase conversions.

Conversion rate optimization (CRO) techniques, such as A/B testing, user experience analysis, and customer journey mapping, can help businesses identify areas for improvement and implement strategies to increase conversions. By continuously monitoring and optimizing conversion rates, companies can maximize the return on their marketing investments and improve overall sales performance.

It's important to note that CPA and conversion rates are interconnected. Improving conversion rates can positively impact CPA by increasing the number of customers acquired without increasing marketing expenses. Similarly, reducing CPA can result in a more cost-effective customer acquisition strategy, leading to better return on investment and potentially higher conversion rates.

Ultimately, the goal is to achieve a balance between CPA and conversion rates to ensure efficient customer acquisition while maximizing revenue and profitability. By monitoring and optimizing these metrics, businesses can refine their sales and marketing strategies, enhance customer acquisition efforts, and drive sustainable growth in their target markets.

CRM SOFTWARE

Almost all sales functions will require a CRM of some sort. Let's look at some of the CRM systems available and how they are important to managing the sales process.

Customer Relationship Management (CRM) systems are software applications that help businesses manage their interactions and relationships with customers. They provide a centralized platform to store customer data, track communication, and automate various sales and marketing processes. Here are some popular CRM systems and their importance in managing the sales process:

1. Salesforce: Salesforce is one of the most widely used CRM systems. It offers a comprehensive suite of features for managing sales, marketing, customer service, and more. Salesforce provides a centralized database to store customer information, track leads, manage opportunities, and automate sales workflows. It enables sales teams to effectively manage the entire sales process, from lead generation to closing deals, while providing valuable insights and analytics to drive sales performance.

2. HubSpot CRM: HubSpot CRM is a popular choice for small to medium-sized businesses. It offers a user-friendly interface and a range of sales and marketing tools. HubSpot CRM allows businesses to organize contacts, track deals, and automate sales processes. It also integrates with other HubSpot tools, such as marketing automation and customer service, providing a holistic view of customer interactions and enabling seamless collaboration across teams.

3. Zoho CRM: Zoho CRM is known for its affordability and flexibility. It provides features to manage sales, marketing, customer support, and more. Zoho CRM allows businesses to track leads, manage pipelines, and automate sales activities. It also offers integrations with other Zoho applications, as well as third-party tools, providing a customizable and scalable CRM solution for businesses of all sizes.

4. Microsoft Dynamics 365: Microsoft Dynamics 365 is a comprehensive CRM and ERP (Enterprise Resource Planning) solution. It offers robust sales management capabilities, including lead and opportunity management, sales forecasting, and analytics. Microsoft Dynamics 365 integrates with other Microsoft products, such as Outlook and Excel, providing a seamless experience for sales teams. It also offers scalability and customization options to meet the unique needs of different industries and business sizes.

32 A CRM System will be a key system in most businesses

5. Pipedrive: Pipedrive is a CRM system designed specifically for sales teams. It focuses on pipeline management, deal tracking, and sales performance analytics. Pipedrive offers a visual and intuitive interface, making it easy for sales professionals to track leads, manage deals, and prioritize tasks. It also integrates with various third-party tools, allowing businesses to customize their CRM workflow according to their specific requirements.

The importance of CRM systems in managing the sales process:

1. Centralized Customer Database: CRM systems provide a centralized repository to store customer data, including contact information, communication history, and purchase details. This enables sales teams to have a comprehensive view of each customer, facilitating personalized and targeted sales interactions.

2. Lead Management and Tracking: CRM systems help manage leads effectively by tracking their progress through the sales funnel. Sales teams can prioritize leads, assign tasks, and track follow-ups, ensuring that no potential sales opportunity is missed.

3. Sales Process Automation: CRM systems automate repetitive sales tasks, such as lead nurturing, email communication, and deal tracking. This saves time and allows sales professionals to focus on building relationships and closing deals.

4. Sales Analytics and Reporting: CRM systems provide valuable insights and analytics on sales performance, pipeline health, and customer behaviour. Sales managers can

analyse data to identify trends, measure sales effectiveness, and make informed decisions to improve overall sales performance.

5. Collaboration and Communication: CRM systems enable collaboration and communication within sales teams and across departments. Sales professionals can easily share information, collaborate on deals, and align their efforts to provide a seamless customer experience.

6. Customer Segmentation and Personalization: CRM systems allow businesses to segment customers based on various criteria, such as demographics, purchase history, or behaviour. This segmentation enables targeted marketing and personalized sales approaches, increasing the chances of converting leads into customers.

CRM systems are essential tools for managing the sales process. They streamline sales activities, provide valuable insights, and improve customer relationships, ultimately leading to increased sales efficiency, higher customer satisfaction, and business growth. The choice of CRM system depends on the specific needs and goals of the business, as well as factors such as budget, scalability, and integrations with existing tools.

LEAD GENERATION

Lead generation is the process of identifying and attracting potential customers (leads) who have expressed interest in your products or services. Some methods include:

1. Content Marketing: Create and distribute valuable, informative, and engaging content through blog posts, articles, videos, ebooks, or webinars. Offer this content as gated resources, where prospects need to provide their contact information to access it.

2. Search Engine Optimization (SEO): Optimize your website and content to rank higher in search engine results. Use relevant keywords, create high-quality content, and build backlinks to improve organic visibility and attract potential leads.

3. Pay-per-Click (PPC) Advertising: Use platforms like Google Ads or social media advertising (e.g., Facebook Ads) to display targeted ads to potential customers. Set up campaigns with relevant keywords and demographics to drive traffic to specific landing pages and capture leads.

4. Social Media Marketing: Leverage social media platforms (e.g., Facebook, LinkedIn, Instagram, Twitter) to engage with your target audience. Share valuable content, participate in discussions, and use targeted ads to reach potential leads.

5. Email Marketing: Build an email list of prospects by offering valuable content, promotions, or newsletters. Nurture these leads with personalized and relevant emails to move them further along the sales funnel.

6. Referral Programs: Encourage satisfied customers to refer your business to their network. Offer incentives such as discounts, rewards, or exclusive access to encourage referrals and generate leads through word-of-mouth.

7. Webinars and Events: Host webinars or participate in industry events to showcase your expertise, provide value to attendees, and capture leads through registrations or contact forms.

8. Networking and Partnerships: Attend industry conferences, seminars, or local networking events to establish connections with potential leads and industry influencers. Collaborate with complementary businesses or professionals to cross-promote and generate leads.

9. Lead Magnets: Offer valuable resources, such as free guides, templates, checklists, or toolkits, in exchange for contact information. These lead magnets incentivize prospects to provide their details and become leads.

10. Direct Outreach: Reach out to potential leads directly through personalized emails, cold calling, or social media messaging. Tailor your messages to address their pain points and offer solutions that can drive interest and engagement.

11. Content Syndication: Repurpose and distribute your content through third-party platforms, industry publications, or guest blogging. This exposes your brand to a wider audience and generates leads from different sources.

12. Live Chat on Website: Implement live chat functionality on your website to engage with visitors in real-time. Collect contact information and answer their queries promptly to convert them into leads.

13. Lead Generation Forms: Optimize your website with lead capture forms strategically placed on landing pages or blog posts. Keep the forms simple and ask for minimal information to encourage conversions.

14. Customer Referrals: Encourage existing customers to refer their contacts by offering referral incentives or rewards. Satisfied customers can be powerful advocates and a valuable source of new leads.

15. Analyse and Optimize: Continuously track and analyse lead generation efforts to identify the most effective channels, content, and strategies. Use data-driven insights to optimize your lead generation campaigns and improve results over time.

Remember, an effective lead generation strategy often involves a combination of these methods tailored to your target audience, industry, and specific business goals. Experiment, measure results, and refine your approach to generate a steady stream of qualified leads for your sales efforts.

Don't delay with sales leads. A frequent fault in the sales process is the speed with which reps will chase up on fresh leads. It is important that high priority leads are chased up as soon as possible. So many sales are lost by being slow out of the gate when following up high priority leads.

UPSELLING

Upselling is the practice of encouraging customers to purchase a higher-end or upgraded version of a product or service, or additional related products, with the aim of increasing the overall value of the sale. There are many reasons for prioritising this:

1. Increased Revenue: Upselling can significantly boost revenue and profitability. By convincing customers to upgrade to a higher-priced product or add complementary items, businesses can increase the average transaction value. This allows for greater revenue generation without acquiring new customers or incurring significant additional costs.

2. Enhanced Customer Satisfaction: Upselling can improve customer satisfaction by offering them more value and better solutions. By recommending products or services that meet their specific needs, customers perceive that you understand and care about their requirements. This enhances their overall experience and increases their likelihood of repeat purchases and positive word-of-mouth referrals.

3. Long-term Customer Relationship Building: Upselling provides an opportunity to deepen customer relationships. By demonstrating your expertise and understanding of their needs, customers are more likely to perceive you as a trusted advisor rather than just a transactional seller. This fosters loyalty, strengthens the relationship, and increases the chances of retaining them as long-term customers.

4. Improved Customer Lifetime Value: Upselling can have a significant impact on the customer lifetime value (CLV). By increasing the value of each transaction, businesses can maximize the revenue generated from each customer over their lifetime. This not only increases short-term profitability but also provides a solid foundation for sustainable business growth.

5. Competitive Advantage: Upselling allows businesses to differentiate themselves from competitors. By offering upgraded or premium options, businesses can position themselves as providers of higher-quality products or services. This can help attract customers who value the additional benefits and features offered, even if they come at a higher price point.

6. Cross-Selling Opportunities: Upselling often goes hand in hand with cross-selling. When engaging in an upsell conversation, businesses can also present complementary products or services that enhance the customer's overall experience or address related needs. This can lead to additional sales and further diversification of revenue streams.

34 Maximise the revenue you can get from your existing customer base

7. Increased Product Adoption: Upselling can encourage customers to fully utilize and experience the benefits of more advanced or feature-rich products. By highlighting the added value and capabilities of the upgraded version, businesses can increase the likelihood of customers fully

leveraging the product's potential. This not only enhances customer satisfaction but also reduces the risk of churn.

8. Cost-Effective Marketing: Upselling is a cost-effective strategy compared to acquiring new customers. It leverages the existing customer base and resources, allowing businesses to focus their marketing efforts on customers who have already shown interest and trust. This can result in a higher return on investment (ROI) as compared to acquiring new customers through expensive marketing campaigns.

It is important to approach upselling with a customer-centric mindset. The focus should be on genuinely understanding the customer's needs and recommending products or services that genuinely add value to their experience. By doing so, businesses can create win-win situations where customers benefit from enhanced solutions, and businesses achieve their revenue and growth objectives.

CROSS SELLING

Cross-selling is a sales technique where a business encourages customers to purchase additional products or services that complement or enhance their initial purchase. It involves recommending related or complementary items that provide value or meet additional needs. Like upselling, it is similarly important:

1. Increased Revenue: Cross-selling can significantly boost revenue by increasing the average transaction value. By

suggesting additional products or services, businesses can capitalize on the customer's existing interest and willingness to buy. This leads to higher sales volume and overall profitability.

2. Enhanced Customer Satisfaction: Cross-selling offers customers the opportunity to discover and purchase related products or services that enhance their initial purchase. By recommending items that are relevant and valuable, businesses can provide a more comprehensive solution to customers' needs, thereby increasing their satisfaction and loyalty.

3. Improved Customer Engagement: Cross-selling allows businesses to engage customers in meaningful conversations and interactions. By understanding their preferences and needs, businesses can offer personalized recommendations and demonstrate a deeper understanding of their requirements. This builds trust and strengthens the customer-business relationship.

4. Upside for Customers: Cross-selling can benefit customers by offering them products or services that complement their original purchase. It saves them time and effort in searching for additional solutions and helps them discover related items they may not have been aware of. Customers appreciate businesses that anticipate their needs and provide convenient options.

5. Increased Customer Lifetime Value: Cross-selling contributes to increasing the customer lifetime value (CLV). By offering relevant add-ons or complementary products, businesses can maximize the revenue generated from each customer over their entire relationship. This extends the

customer's value to the business and improves long-term profitability.

6. Market Penetration: Cross-selling enables businesses to penetrate deeper into their target market. By promoting a range of related products or services, businesses can reach a broader customer base and increase market share. This can help them expand their presence and compete more effectively within their industry.

7. Brand Loyalty and Advocacy: Successful cross-selling initiatives can foster brand loyalty and advocacy. When customers have positive experiences with cross-sold products that enhance their original purchase, they are more likely to become loyal supporters of the brand. Satisfied customers may also recommend the business to others, leading to new customer acquisitions through word-of-mouth.

8. Inventory Optimization: Cross-selling allows businesses to manage inventory effectively. By promoting complementary products or services, businesses can ensure a balanced distribution of sales across their offerings. This helps prevent inventory imbalances and reduces the risk of overstocking or underutilizing certain products.

9. Competitive Advantage: Effective cross-selling strategies can differentiate a business from its competitors. By offering a comprehensive range of related products or services, businesses can position themselves as a one-stop solution provider. This can attract customers who appreciate the convenience and comprehensive nature of the offerings.

10. Data and Insights: Cross-selling initiatives provide valuable data and insights about customer behaviour and

preferences. By analysing customer purchase patterns and preferences for cross-sold items, businesses can gain a deeper understanding of their target audience. This information can inform product development, marketing strategies, and future cross-selling opportunities.

When implementing cross-selling, businesses should focus on understanding their customers' needs, providing relevant recommendations, and maintaining transparency and trust. By offering valuable and complementary options, businesses can create a positive customer experience and drive additional revenue growth.

THE IMPORTANCE OF A SALES SCRIPT

A sales script is a structured outline or guide that sales representatives use during customer interactions to ensure consistent and effective communication. You will hear this again, selling is a science. Some considerations:

1. Consistency: A sales script provides a consistent framework for sales representatives to follow. It ensures that key messages, product information, and value propositions are consistently communicated to customers. This consistency helps maintain a unified brand image and prevents variations in messaging across different sales interactions.

2. Message Clarity: A well-crafted sales script ensures that the sales message is clear, concise, and impactful. It helps sales representatives articulate the features, benefits, and

unique selling points of the product or service in a way that resonates with the target audience. A clear and compelling message increases the chances of capturing customer interest and generating positive responses.

3. Overcoming Objections: Sales scripts are designed to address common objections or concerns that customers may have. They provide sales representatives with prepared responses and strategies to overcome objections effectively. Having well-thought-out answers helps build credibility, overcome customer scepticism, and increases the likelihood of closing a sale.

4. Training and Onboarding: Sales scripts serve as valuable training tools for new sales team members. They provide a structured framework for learning the sales process, product knowledge, and effective communication techniques. Sales scripts enable new hires to quickly grasp the key selling points and confidently engage with customers.

5. Time Efficiency: A sales script helps streamline sales interactions and saves time for both the sales representative and the customer. By providing a structured flow of the conversation, a sales script ensures that important information is conveyed efficiently. This allows sales representatives to cover all essential points within a reasonable timeframe, increasing productivity and optimizing customer engagement.

6. Customization and Personalization: While a sales script provides a framework, it can also be customized and personalized based on individual customer needs and preferences. Sales representatives can adapt the script to align with the specific situation and tailor their

communication to each customer. This ensures that the sales pitch feels more personalized and relevant, enhancing the customer experience.

35 *Selling is a science. Prepare and analyse all stages of the process.*

7. Confidence and Preparedness: Having a sales script empowers sales representatives with confidence and preparedness during customer interactions. It reduces anxiety and uncertainty by providing a roadmap for the conversation. Sales representatives who are well-versed in the script are better equipped to handle objections, answer questions, and steer the conversation towards a successful outcome.

8. Metrics and Analysis: Sales scripts allow businesses to measure and analyse sales performance more effectively. By using standardized scripts, businesses can compare the effectiveness of different approaches, test variations, and track outcomes. This data-driven approach helps identify areas for improvement, refine sales strategies, and optimize conversion rates.

9. Scalability and Replicability: Sales scripts are particularly valuable in organizations with multiple sales representatives. They ensure consistent messaging and sales techniques across the team, making it easier to scale operations and maintain a cohesive sales approach. New hires can quickly adapt to the established script, ensuring continuity and a seamless customer experience.

10. Continuous Improvement: Sales scripts can be regularly reviewed and updated based on customer feedback, market trends, and sales performance data. This allows businesses to continuously refine and improve their sales messaging, techniques, and strategies. Regularly updating the script ensures that it remains relevant, effective, and aligned with the evolving needs and expectations of customers.

While a sales script is a valuable tool, it is important to strike a balance between structure and flexibility. Sales representatives should be encouraged to adapt and personalize the script to suit individual customer interactions while maintaining consistency in key messaging. This helps create a natural and engaging conversation that builds rapport, addresses customer needs, and drives successful sales outcomes.

THE SALES MEETING

Ask leading questions. It makes the potential customer feel you care about their business and challenges. It also helps you to better understand the customer issues and show how you can help solve these.

You should do no more than 40% of the talking. Even though many amateur sales reps will happily rattle off incessantly about how great their product or service is and will barley let the customer get a word in. NOTHING is more off putting.

MAKE SURE from the outset that you are speaking with the decision maker. There is nothing worse than spending weeks on pitching and meetings only to be told that your potential customer now has to bring everything to his or her boss for a final decision. This is one of the most common mistakes people still make.

Put effort in. For example, you might want to mock up a graphic to the potential customer can visualise your product as it would look for their business. People buy with their eyes.

36	*Prepare and put effort into the meeting - People appreciate effort*

37	*Meeting skills - Project your voice. Build confidence and trust. That will help establish trust in your product or service. Dont speak too fast and pause after sentences. Never speak more than 40% of the time at a sales meeting. Show interest in the customer's business and issues. You have 2 ears for a reason!*

DEVELOP BRAND AMBASSADORS

Developing brand ambassadors is a valuable strategy for businesses to leverage the passion and advocacy of loyal customers to promote their brand. So how do you do this?:

1. Identify Your Ideal Ambassadors: Determine the characteristics and qualities you seek in brand ambassadors. Look for customers who are enthusiastic, engaged, and have a genuine affinity for your brand. Consider factors

such as their social influence, online presence, and ability to communicate effectively.

2. Nurture Customer Relationships: Build strong relationships with your customers by providing exceptional experiences, personalized interactions, and exceptional customer service. Focus on exceeding their expectations, listening to their feedback, and addressing their needs promptly. When customers feel valued and connected to your brand, they are more likely to become brand ambassadors.

3. Provide an Outstanding Product or Service: Delivering a high-quality product or service is crucial to developing brand ambassadors. Ensure that your offerings meet or exceed customer expectations and consistently deliver value. When customers have a positive experience with your brand, they are more inclined to share their positive experiences with others.

4. Create a Sense of Community: Foster a community around your brand by creating platforms for customers to connect and engage with each other. This can be through social media groups, forums, or online communities. Encourage conversations, facilitate knowledge sharing, and create opportunities for customers to interact with each other and with your brand.

5. Offer Exclusive Benefits: Provide exclusive benefits, rewards, or incentives to your loyal customers. This can include special discounts, early access to new products or features, or exclusive events. By giving your brand ambassadors unique perks, you strengthen their sense of belonging and encourage them to advocate for your brand.

38   *Nurture and reward brand ambassadors*

6. Encourage User-Generated Content: Encourage brand ambassadors to create and share user-generated content that showcases their experiences with your brand. This can be in the form of reviews, testimonials, social media posts, or blog articles. Acknowledge and amplify their content by sharing it on your official channels, which further strengthens their relationship with your brand.

7. Offer Referral Programs: Implement a referral program that rewards brand ambassadors for referring new customers to your business. Provide incentives such as discounts, credits, or exclusive access to encourage them to spread the word about your brand to their network. This turns brand ambassadors into active advocates who actively promote your brand to others.

8. Engage in Influencer Marketing: Collaborate with influential individuals or micro-influencers in your industry who align with your brand values. These influencers can help amplify your brand message and reach a wider audience. Partnering with influencers who genuinely believe in your brand can generate valuable word-of-mouth and create additional brand ambassadors.

9. Provide Ongoing Support and Recognition: Continue to engage with your brand ambassadors by providing ongoing support, resources, and recognition. Stay in regular communication, offer assistance, and address their questions or concerns promptly. Recognize their efforts through shout-outs, features, or rewards, which reinforces their status as brand ambassadors and motivates them to continue advocating for your brand.

10. Measure and Evaluate Results: Track the impact and effectiveness of your brand ambassador program. Measure metrics such as engagement levels, reach, referral conversions, and overall brand sentiment. Analyse the data to identify areas for improvement, optimize your strategy, and recognize the most influential brand ambassadors.

Remember, developing brand ambassadors is a long-term process that requires consistent effort and genuine relationships with your customers. By focusing on building strong connections, providing exceptional experiences, and offering exclusive benefits, you can cultivate a community of passionate advocates who will champion your brand and contribute to its success.

MINE YOUR CUSTOMER BASE FOR SALES

Mining your customer base for sales involves analysing and leveraging the data and insights you have about your existing customers to identify opportunities for increased sales and improved customer relationships. Here are some steps to effectively do this:

1. Collect and Organize Customer Data: Gather and organize relevant data about your customers, including their contact information, purchase history, preferences, interactions with your brand, and any additional data points that are available to you. This data can be collected through

customer relationship management (CRM) systems, sales records, website analytics, surveys, and other sources.

2. Segment Your Customer Base: Divide your customer base into segments based on shared characteristics such as demographics, purchasing behaviour, preferences, or engagement levels. This segmentation allows you to tailor your sales strategies and messaging to specific customer groups and identify the most valuable segments with the highest potential for sales growth.

3. Analyse Purchase Patterns: Analyse the purchase history of your customers to identify patterns, trends, and opportunities. Look for common product combinations, frequent purchase intervals, or specific products that are popular among certain customer segments. This analysis can reveal cross-selling or upselling opportunities and help you create targeted sales campaigns.

4. Identify High-Value Customers: Identify customers who have a high lifetime value (CLV) or have made significant purchases in the past. These customers are more likely to be receptive to new offers and have a higher potential for upselling or cross-selling. Prioritize engaging with these customers to nurture the relationship and identify opportunities for additional sales.

5. Utilize Data-Driven Marketing: Leverage customer data to create personalized and targeted marketing campaigns. Use customer segmentation and purchase history to deliver relevant product recommendations, personalized offers, or exclusive promotions. Data-driven marketing strategies can increase customer engagement, improve conversion rates, and drive incremental sales.

6. Implement Customer Loyalty Programs: Develop customer loyalty programs that incentivize repeat purchases and referrals. Reward customers for their loyalty and encourage them to engage with your brand on an ongoing basis. Loyalty programs can provide exclusive discounts, access to special events, or other perks that motivate customers to choose your brand over competitors.

7. Provide Exceptional Customer Service: Ensure that your customer service is top-notch and consistently exceeds customer expectations. Promptly address customer inquiries, concerns, or issues to build trust and loyalty. Exceptional customer service can lead to positive word-of-mouth referrals, repeat purchases, and increased sales from satisfied customers.

8. Foster Customer Engagement: Actively engage with your customers through various channels such as social media, email marketing, or personalized follow-ups. Encourage feedback, seek customer opinions, and create opportunities for dialogue. Engaged customers are more likely to make repeat purchases and refer your brand to others.

9. Continuously Monitor and Measure Results: Regularly review and assess the effectiveness of your customer mining efforts. Track key performance indicators (KPIs) such as customer retention rate, customer lifetime value, sales conversion rates, and overall revenue growth. Analyse the data to identify areas for improvement and refine your sales strategies accordingly.

10. Iterate and Optimize: Continuously refine and optimize your customer mining strategies based on insights and feedback from your customer base. Adapt to changing

customer preferences, market dynamics, and industry trends. Continual improvement and adaptation ensure that you stay relevant and maximize sales opportunities within your customer base.

11. Referral programs. Give your customer base incentives for referring you new customers. Maybe they get 2 months free service for every customer they refer. Vary up the offer every other month. It should be part of your ongoing marketing.

By effectively mining your customer base for sales, you can uncover valuable insights, deepen customer relationships, and drive revenue growth. Through data analysis, personalized marketing, customer engagement, and exceptional service, you can tap into the potential of your existing customer base and foster long-term sales success.

39

Existing customer bases are often overlooked but your customers can be great for lead generation with referral programs and should be a key part of your ongoing marketing plan

TOOLS

1. Video Conferencing Platforms: Remote selling has become increasingly important in today's digital age, especially with the rise of remote work and virtual interactions. Video conferencing tools like Zoom, Microsoft Teams, or Google Meet enable face-to-face communication with clients and prospects. These platforms facilitate virtual sales meetings, product demonstrations, and presentations, allowing for real-time interaction and building personal connections despite the physical distance.

2. CRM Systems: We have covered these already. Customer Relationship Management (CRM) software such as Salesforce, HubSpot, or Zoho CRM helps sales teams manage and track customer interactions, leads, and opportunities. CRM systems provide a centralized database for customer information, allowing sales professionals to maintain accurate records, track sales activities, and monitor the progress of deals.

3. Sales Engagement Tools: Sales engagement platforms like Outreach, SalesLoft, or Groove streamline and automate sales workflows, including email outreach, follow-ups, and prospecting. These tools help sales teams optimize their outreach efforts, track email open and response rates, and schedule automated follow-ups, improving efficiency and productivity.

4. Presentation and Demonstration Tools: Tools like PowerPoint, Google Slides, or Prezi are essential for creating compelling presentations and product demonstrations.

These tools allow sales professionals to showcase their products or services, highlight key features and benefits, and visually engage prospects during remote sales interactions.

5. Document Sharing and Collaboration: Cloud storage and collaboration tools such as Google Drive, Dropbox, or Microsoft OneDrive facilitate seamless sharing and collaboration on sales documents, proposals, and contracts. These platforms enable real-time editing, version control, and secure file sharing, ensuring smooth collaboration with clients and team members.

6. E-Signature Solutions: E-signature platforms like DocuSign, Adobe Sign, or HelloSign simplify the process of obtaining legally binding signatures remotely. These tools eliminate the need for physical paperwork and allow sales professionals to send contracts, proposals, and agreements electronically, enabling a faster and more efficient sales process.

7. Sales Analytics and Reporting: Analytics tools like Tableau, Google Analytics, or Microsoft Power BI provide valuable insights into sales performance, customer behaviour, and lead generation. These tools help sales teams analyse data, track key performance metrics, and generate reports, enabling data-driven decision-making and identifying areas for improvement.

8. Virtual Sales Enablement Platforms: Sales enablement tools such as Highspot, Seismic, or Showpad offer centralized platforms for organizing and accessing sales collateral, product information, and training materials. These platforms empower remote sales teams with easy access to relevant content, ensuring they have the right resources to engage prospects effectively.

9. Online Payment and Invoicing Systems: Online payment platforms like PayPal, Stripe, or Square enable secure and convenient payment processing for remote sales transactions. These tools streamline the payment process, provide flexibility for customers, and help sales professionals close deals quickly.

10. Virtual Networking and Social Selling: Social media platforms such as LinkedIn, Twitter, or Instagram can be leveraged for virtual networking and social selling. Sales professionals can connect with prospects, share valuable content, participate in industry discussions, and build relationships online, expanding their reach and establishing credibility.

By leveraging these tools and technologies, remote sales teams can effectively engage with prospects, deliver compelling presentations, track sales activities, collaborate with clients, and streamline the sales process. Investing in the right tools and continuously adapting to emerging technologies can enhance remote selling capabilities and drive sales success.

DEVELOPING SALES CHANNELS

Developing sales channels on platforms like Amazon and eBay can provide businesses with access to a wider customer base and increased sales opportunities. Some key steps to consider when developing your sales channel:

1. Research and Understand the Platforms: Begin by familiarizing yourself with the rules, guidelines, and selling policies of each platform. Understand the fee structures, product categories, and target audience of Amazon and eBay. Conduct market research to assess the competition, identify popular products, and evaluate the demand for your offerings on these platforms.

2. Optimize Product Listings: Create compelling and optimized product listings on Amazon and eBay. Use high-quality images, accurate product descriptions, and relevant keywords to improve visibility and attract potential buyers. Pay attention to factors like pricing, shipping options, and customer reviews to enhance the appeal of your listings.

3. Fulfilment Options: Decide on the fulfilment method that best suits your business. Amazon offers Fulfilment by Amazon (FBA), where they handle storage, packaging, and shipping, while eBay provides various fulfilment options, including self-fulfilment or third-party fulfilment services. Choose the option that aligns with your business capabilities and customer expectations.

4. Pricing and Promotions: Set competitive pricing for your products on these platforms, taking into account fees and commissions. Consider offering promotional discounts or

running special deals to attract customers and encourage repeat purchases. Monitor competitor pricing and adjust your strategy accordingly to stay competitive in the marketplace.

5. Customer Service: Provide excellent customer service on these platforms to build trust and positive feedback. Respond promptly to customer inquiries, address concerns, and handle returns or refunds professionally. Positive reviews and ratings play a significant role in establishing credibility and attracting more customers.

6. Inventory Management: Efficiently manage your inventory to avoid stockouts or overstocking. Utilize inventory management tools or software to keep track of stock levels, monitor sales velocity, and replenish inventory in a timely manner. This ensures a smooth selling experience and minimizes the risk of losing sales due to unavailability.

7. Marketing and Advertising: Leverage the marketing and advertising features available on Amazon and eBay to promote your products. Utilize sponsored product ads, targeted campaigns, and other advertising options to increase visibility and reach a wider audience. Optimize your listings with relevant keywords to improve search rankings and organic visibility.

8. Monitor and Optimize Performance: Regularly monitor your sales performance, customer feedback, and key metrics provided by the platforms. Analyse data on sales volume, conversion rates, customer satisfaction, and return rates. Identify areas for improvement and make data-driven decisions to optimize your sales strategy and enhance your presence on these platforms.

9. Expand and Diversify: Once you establish a successful presence on Amazon and eBay, consider expanding to other sales channels, such as other online marketplaces or your own e-commerce website. Diversifying your sales channels helps mitigate risks and expands your reach to a broader customer base.

10. Stay Informed and Adapt: Keep up with platform updates, policy changes, and industry trends. Stay informed about new features, tools, or opportunities that the platforms offer. Continuously adapt your strategies, product offerings, and customer engagement tactics to stay competitive in the evolving e-commerce landscape.

Developing sales channels on platforms like Amazon and eBay requires careful planning, optimization, and ongoing effort. By utilizing the features and resources provided by these platforms, businesses can tap into a large customer base, drive sales growth, and increase brand visibility in the online marketplace.

40 Test different Sales Channels to see which work best

BUILD A SALES FUNNELL SPECIFIC TO YOUR BUSINESS

Building a sales funnel specific to your business involves understanding your target audience, mapping out the customer journey, and implementing effective strategies to guide prospects through each stage of the funnel.

1. Define Your Target Audience: Clearly identify your target audience and understand their demographics, needs, preferences, and pain points. This will help you tailor your messaging and offerings to resonate with your ideal customers.

2. Map the Customer Journey: Visualize the different stages that your prospects go through before making a purchase. Typically, a sales funnel consists of awareness, interest, consideration, and decision stages. Map out the touchpoints and interactions that occur at each stage.

3. Create Awareness: Attract potential customers by implementing marketing strategies that increase brand visibility and awareness. This can include content marketing, social media advertising, search engine optimization (SEO), influencer collaborations, or paid advertising. The goal is to generate leads and capture the attention of your target audience.

4. Capture Leads: Offer valuable content or incentives to capture leads' contact information, such as email addresses. This can be done through lead magnets like e-books, whitepapers, webinars, or gated content. Build a landing

page or opt-in form to collect leads and start nurturing the relationship.

5. Nurture Prospects: Develop a lead nurturing strategy to engage with your leads and build trust. This can involve sending targeted emails, providing valuable content through newsletters or drip campaigns, or offering personalized recommendations based on their interests and needs. The goal is to keep your brand top-of-mind and educate prospects about the value your product or service offers.

6. Convert Leads into Customers: When leads show interest and engagement, it's time to guide them towards making a purchase. Offer product demonstrations, free trials, or consultations to showcase the value of your offering. Use persuasive messaging and compelling calls-to-action (CTAs) to encourage conversions.

7. Close the Sale: Implement effective sales strategies to close the deal. This can involve personalized sales calls, negotiation, proposal presentations, or special offers. Address any concerns or objections prospects may have and provide a seamless purchasing experience.

8. Upsell and Cross-sell: After a successful sale, leverage the opportunity to upsell or cross-sell additional products or services. Offer complementary or upgraded options that enhance the value for the customer. This increases customer satisfaction and maximizes revenue per customer.

9. Retain and Delight Customers: Focus on providing exceptional post-purchase experiences to foster customer loyalty and encourage repeat purchases. Implement customer retention strategies such as loyalty programs,

exclusive offers, personalized communication, and outstanding customer support.

10. Measure and Optimize: Continuously monitor and analyse the performance of your sales funnel. Track key metrics such as conversion rates, customer acquisition costs, customer lifetime value, and sales revenue. Identify bottlenecks or areas of improvement and make data-driven adjustments to optimize your funnel over time.

Remember, building a sales funnel specific to your business requires a deep understanding of your target audience, continuous optimization, and adaptation based on customer feedback and market trends. By aligning your strategies with the customer journey and providing a seamless and personalized experience, you can effectively guide prospects through the funnel and drive sales growth for your business.

Like every other aspect of business, there should be a systematic approach to sales.

 **41** *Again, selling is a science. Make sure you are on top of the various stages of the sales funnel.*

NOTES

NOTES

CHAPTER
5

MARKETING

THE COMPANY WEBSITE

HAVING A GREAT COMPANY website is vitally important from a marketing perspective, regardless of whether or not you are selling online. Why is this?:

1. Online Presence and Branding: A company website serves as the online representation of your brand. It is often the first point of contact for potential customers and plays a crucial role in shaping their perception of your business. A well-designed and professional website helps establish credibility, build trust, and create a positive brand image.

2. Information Hub: Your website serves as a central hub for all information related to your products, services, and company. It provides a platform to showcase your offerings, communicate your value proposition, and highlight your unique selling points. A well-organized and informative website helps educate potential customers and facilitates their decision-making process.

3. Increased Reach and Accessibility: With the increasing use of the internet and digital devices, a website allows you to reach a broader audience beyond geographical limitations. It enables potential customers from anywhere in the world to access information about your business, increasing your visibility and potential customer base.

4. Lead Generation and Conversion: A well-optimized website can be an effective tool for lead generation and conversion. By incorporating lead capture forms, call-to-action buttons, and clear contact information, you can encourage visitors to

take action and provide their contact details. This allows you to capture leads and nurture them into potential customers.

5. Enhanced Customer Experience: A great website provides an intuitive and user-friendly experience for visitors. It allows them to easily navigate through different sections, find the information they need, and interact with your brand. A positive user experience leads to increased engagement, longer visit durations, and higher chances of conversion.

6. Showcasing Expertise and Thought Leadership: Your website can be a platform to demonstrate your expertise and establish yourself as a thought leader in your industry. Through blog posts, articles, case studies, and whitepapers, you can share valuable insights, industry trends, and solutions to customer pain points. This helps build credibility and positions your business as a trusted authority.

7. Integration with Other Marketing Channels: Your website serves as a central hub that integrates with other marketing channels. It can be linked to your social media profiles, email marketing campaigns, online advertising, and other digital channels. This synergy helps reinforce your marketing messages and provides a cohesive and integrated customer experience.

8. Analytics and Data Insights: With the right tools, your website allows you to gather valuable data and insights about your visitors. Analytics platforms like Google Analytics provide data on website traffic, user behaviour, conversion rates, and more. This data helps you understand the effectiveness of your marketing efforts, identify areas for improvement, and make data-driven decisions.

9. Scalability and Adaptability: A website provides scalability and adaptability for your marketing efforts. You can easily update and modify content, add new features, and incorporate emerging technologies to stay current and relevant. This flexibility allows you to adapt to changing customer needs and market trends.

10. Competitive Advantage: In today's digital landscape, a great website is not just a nice-to-have, but a necessity. Many of your competitors are likely investing in their online presence, and having a subpar or non-existent website can put you at a disadvantage. A well-designed and optimized website can differentiate you from competitors, attract more customers, and contribute to your overall marketing success.

A great company website is an essential marketing tool that enhances your online presence, establishes your brand, generates leads, provides valuable information, and facilitates customer engagement. It is a powerful asset that helps you stand out from the competition, build credibility, and drive business growth.

42 *The company website helps many aspects of the business – sales, marketing, brand confidence, SEO, and ultimately should reflect the quality of the company's product or service.*

ONLINE

Marketing your business online opens up a world of opportunities to reach a wider audience, build brand awareness, and drive growth.

Let's look at some of the ways to do this. Depending on your industry/product or service, many of these may not be applicable but it is crucial you understand what the internet has to offer no matter what.

1. Search Engine Optimization (SEO): Implementing SEO techniques helps improve your website's visibility in search engine results. By optimizing your website's structure, content, and keywords, you can increase organic traffic and attract relevant users actively searching for products or services like yours.

2. Pay-Per-Click (PPC) Advertising: PPC advertising platforms like Google Ads and Bing Ads allow you to create targeted ads that appear in search engine results or on relevant websites. With PPC, you pay only when users click on your ad. This method provides immediate visibility and control over your budget, allowing you to reach your target audience effectively.

3. Social Media Marketing: Social media platforms like Facebook, Instagram, Twitter, LinkedIn, and YouTube offer powerful marketing opportunities. By creating engaging content, running targeted ads, and fostering relationships with your audience, you can increase brand awareness, drive traffic to your website, and generate leads.

4. Content Marketing: Creating valuable and relevant content, such as blog posts, articles, videos, infographics, and ebooks, establishes your expertise and builds trust with your audience. Content marketing helps drive organic traffic, improve search engine rankings, and engage and educate your target audience.

5. Email Marketing: Building an email list and implementing email marketing campaigns allows you to nurture leads and maintain a direct line of communication with your audience. By sending personalized and engaging emails, you can promote your products or services, share valuable content, and drive conversions and repeat business.

6. Influencer Marketing: Collaborating with influencers or industry experts who have a significant following can help amplify your brand's reach and credibility. By leveraging their influence and audience, you can tap into their followers' trust and increase brand visibility, generating more leads and conversions.

 **43** *Send regular and scheduled emails. Mix in some interesting content with a customer offer. It is a very cheap and still effective form or marketing.*

7. Affiliate Marketing: Partnering with affiliates who promote your products or services in exchange for a commission can be a cost-effective way to expand your reach. Affiliates drive traffic to your website and earn a commission for each successful referral or sale they generate.

8. Online PR and Media Relations: Building relationships with relevant online publications, bloggers, and journalists can help you secure media coverage, mentions, and backlinks to your website. Online PR helps increase brand visibility, enhances your reputation, and drives targeted traffic.

9. Online Directories and Review Sites: Listing your business in online directories and review sites, such as Google My Business, Yelp, and industry-specific directories, improves your online presence and allows potential customers to find and evaluate your business. Positive reviews and ratings can significantly impact your credibility and attract new customers.

10. Webinars and Online Events: Hosting webinars, online workshops, or virtual events allows you to showcase your expertise, educate your audience, and generate leads. Interactive online events provide an opportunity to engage with potential customers, answer questions, and establish a connection.

 **44** *Hold Sales Webinars to present your products to many potential customers at once. Efficient and lox cost*

11. Remarketing and Retargeting: By using remarketing or retargeting techniques, you can target users who have previously visited your website or interacted with your brand. By showing them relevant ads across various platforms, you can remind them of your products or services and encourage them to convert.

12. Mobile Marketing: With the increasing use of smartphones, mobile marketing is crucial. Optimize your website and marketing campaigns for mobile devices, and consider utilizing SMS marketing, mobile apps, or location-based targeting to reach mobile users effectively.

13. Video Marketing: Videos are highly engaging and shareable content formats. Creating video content for platforms like YouTube, social media, or your website can help you communicate your brand message, showcase your products or services, and connect with your audience on a more personal level.

14. Online Partnerships and Collaborations: Partnering with complementary businesses or industry influencers can help you expand your reach and tap into new customer segments. By cross promoting each other's products or services, you can leverage existing audiences and generate mutual benefits.

15. Data Analytics and Testing: Utilize web analytics tools like Google Analytics to track and analyse the performance of your online marketing efforts. By monitoring key metrics, conducting A/B testing, and making data-driven decisions, you can optimize your strategies for better results.

Remember, an effective online marketing strategy often involves a combination of these methods, tailored to your specific business goals, target audience, and industry. Regularly evaluate your performance, adapt to market trends, and refine your approach to maximize your online marketing efforts and drive business growth.

45 *Partnerships can be good for sales with the correct partner but are also great for brand confidence and can add an underlying monetary value to the business.*

A CRASH COURSE IN GOOGLE ADWORDS

Google AdWords, now known as Google Ads, is an online advertising platform that allows businesses to display ads on Google search results pages, partner websites, and mobile apps. It is a powerful tool for reaching potential customers, increasing website traffic, and driving conversions.

1. Account Setup: Start by creating a Google Ads account and setting up your billing information. Define your campaign goals, such as increasing website visits, generating leads, or driving online sales.

2. Campaign Structure: Google Ads is organized into campaigns, ad groups, and ads. A campaign is a high-level container for your advertising efforts, while ad groups group related keywords and ads together. Create separate campaigns and ad groups based on your products, services, or target audience.

3. Keyword Research: Conduct thorough keyword research to identify relevant search terms that potential customers might use to find your products or services. Use Google's

Keyword Planner tool or other keyword research tools to discover keywords with high search volume and relevance to your business.

4. Ad Formats: Google Ads offers various ad formats, including text ads, display ads, shopping ads, video ads, and app ads. Choose the ad format that aligns with your campaign goals and the preferences of your target audience.

5. Ad Copy: Craft compelling and relevant ad copy that grabs attention, highlights your unique selling points, and encourages users to click. Use ad extensions to provide additional information, such as site links, callouts, or phone numbers, which can enhance your ad's visibility and appeal.

6. Bidding and Budgeting: Determine your bidding strategy and set a budget for your campaigns. Google Ads offers different bidding options, including cost-per-click (CPC), cost-per-thousand impressions (CPM), and target cost-per-acquisition (CPA). Adjust your bids based on your campaign goals and the competitiveness of your keywords.

7. Targeting: Refine your targeting options to reach the most relevant audience. Choose geographic targeting to focus on specific locations, demographic targeting to reach specific age groups or genders, and audience targeting to reach users with specific interests or behaviours.

8. Ad Quality and Relevance: Google values ad quality and relevance. Ensure that your landing pages align with your ad copy and provide a seamless user experience. Optimize your landing pages for speed, mobile-friendliness, and relevant content to improve your ad's quality score and ad rank.

9. Conversion Tracking: Implement conversion tracking to measure the success of your campaigns. Define the desired actions you want users to take, such as form submissions or purchases, and set up conversion tracking codes on your website. This allows you to track and analyse the performance of your ads and optimize accordingly.

10. Monitoring and Optimization: Regularly monitor your campaigns, ad performance, and key metrics. Make data-driven decisions based on performance insights. Adjust your bids, ad copy, and targeting settings to improve campaign performance and maximize your return on investment (ROI).

11. Testing and Experimentation: Continuously test different ad variations, landing pages, and targeting settings to identify what works best for your business. Conduct A/B tests to compare the performance of different elements and optimize your campaigns based on the results.

12. Continuous Learning: Stay updated with the latest Google Ads features, trends, and best practices. Leverage Google Ads resources, attend webinars, and join online communities to enhance your knowledge and skills in running successful Google Ads campaigns.

While this provides an overview of Google Ads, mastering the platform takes time, practice, and ongoing optimization. Experiment, learn from your campaigns, and refine your strategies to drive targeted traffic, increase conversions, and achieve your advertising goals using Google Ads.

A CRASH COURSE IN FACEBOOK ADVERTISING

Facebook Advertising is a powerful platform for businesses to reach their target audience, build brand awareness, and drive conversions.

1. Business Manager: Start by creating a Facebook Business Manager account. This centralizes your advertising efforts, allows you to manage multiple ad accounts, and provides access to additional tools and features.

2. Ad Campaign Objectives: Facebook offers a range of campaign objectives, such as brand awareness, reach, engagement, traffic, conversions, and more. Choose the objective that aligns with your marketing goals.

3. Audience Targeting: Facebook allows precise audience targeting based on demographics, interests, behaviours, and connections. Define your target audience based on factors like age, gender, location, interests, and purchase behaviour to ensure your ads reach the right people.

4. Ad Formats: Facebook offers various ad formats, including image ads, video ads, carousel ads, slideshow ads, and

collection ads. Select the ad format that suits your campaign goals and best showcases your products or services.

5. Compelling Ad Content: Create visually appealing ad content with attention-grabbing headlines, engaging images or videos, and concise, compelling copy. Ensure your ad content aligns with your campaign objective and resonates with your target audience.

6. Ad Placement: Facebook offers different ad placement options, including the Facebook News Feed, Instagram, Audience Network, and Messenger. Choose the placements that are most likely to reach your target audience effectively.

7. Budgeting and Bidding: Set a budget for your campaigns and choose a bidding strategy. Facebook offers options like cost-per-click (CPC), cost-per-thousand impressions (CPM), and cost-per-action (CPA). Adjust your bids based on your campaign goals and performance.

8. Pixel Tracking: Install the Facebook Pixel on your website to track user behaviour, conversions, and optimize your ads. The pixel helps you measure the effectiveness of your ads, retarget website visitors, and create lookalike audiences.

9. Ad Testing and Optimization: Continuously test different ad variations, targeting options, and placements to optimize your campaigns. Monitor key metrics such as click-through rates (CTR), engagement rates, and conversions. Make data-driven decisions and adjust your ads and targeting accordingly.

10. Remarketing and Custom Audiences: Utilize Facebook's remarketing feature to target users who have already interacted with your website or Facebook page. Create

custom audiences based on specific actions, such as website visits, email list subscribers, or app users, to deliver tailored ads to a more receptive audience.

11. Ad Performance Analysis: Use Facebook Ads Manager to analyse campaign performance, including reach, engagement, conversions, and return on ad spend (ROAS). Gain insights into your audience, ad creative, and targeting to optimize your future campaigns.

12. Ongoing Learning: Stay updated with Facebook's ad policies, features, and best practices. Explore Facebook Blueprint, an online learning platform offering courses and certifications to enhance your knowledge and skills in Facebook Advertising.

Remember, successful Facebook Advertising requires continuous learning, testing, and optimization. Stay creative, analyse your results, and adapt your strategies to maximize the impact of your Facebook ads and achieve your marketing objectives.

47

Boost interesting content on Facebook. It can often outperform straight forward ads. Create numbered lists. People love lists. I.e., if you are selling Alarm Systems create an article – 5 Reasons your business needs an Alarm System.

10 THINGS TO DO TO HELP ORGANIC SEARCH

1. Keyword Research: Conduct thorough keyword research to identify relevant keywords and phrases that your target audience is searching for. Use tools like Google Keyword Planner or third-party tools to discover high-volume and low-competition keywords.

2. On-Page Optimization: Optimize your website's pages for search engines. This includes optimizing title tags, meta descriptions, headers, and URL structures. Incorporate relevant keywords naturally into your content and ensure your website is easily crawlable by search engine bots.

3. High-Quality Content: Create valuable, informative, and engaging content that addresses the needs and interests of your target audience. Publish regular blog posts, articles, guides, and other forms of content that provide value and encourage users to stay longer on your website.

4. Page Speed Optimization: Improve your website's loading speed to enhance user experience and satisfy Google's algorithm. Compress images, minify code, enable browser caching, and utilize content delivery networks (CDNs) to speed up your website's performance.

5. Mobile-Friendliness: With most searches now occurring on mobile devices, it's crucial to have a mobile-friendly website. Ensure your website is responsive and displays properly on various screen sizes. Use Google's Mobile-Friendly Test to identify any issues and make necessary improvements.

6. Secure Website (HTTPS): Switch to HTTPS to ensure your website is secure and encrypted. HTTPS is a ranking signal and provides a more trustworthy experience for users. Obtain an SSL certificate for your website and redirect all HTTP URLs to their HTTPS counterparts.

7. Link Building: Earn high-quality backlinks from reputable websites in your industry. Focus on creating compelling content that naturally attracts links. Reach out to influencers, industry blogs, and relevant websites to request backlinks or guest posting opportunities.

8. Local SEO: If you have a physical location or serve a specific geographic area, optimize your website for local searches. Claim and optimize your Google My Business listing, include location-specific keywords in your content, and gather positive reviews from satisfied customers.

9. User Experience (UX): Ensure your website provides a seamless and user-friendly experience. Improve navigation, make information easily accessible, and optimize your website's structure. Enhance user engagement with clear calls-to-action and intuitive design.

10. Regular Monitoring and Analysis: Regularly monitor your website's performance using tools like Google Analytics and Google Search Console. Analyse metrics such as organic traffic, bounce rate, click-through rate (CTR), and keyword rankings. Use these insights to identify areas for improvement and adjust your strategies accordingly.

Remember, organic search optimization is an ongoing process that requires consistent effort and adaptation. Stay up to date with Google's algorithm updates and industry best practices to ensure your website remains visible and ranks well in organic search results.

Spending time and effort in SEO will provide value in the mid-long term. Factor it in to you plans and don't be disheartened if results are slow.

MARKETING THROUGH CONTENT AND INFLUENCE

We have touched on this previously. Marketing your business through content and influence involves leveraging valuable content and collaborating with influential individuals to reach your target audience and build brand awareness.

Define Your Target Audience: Understand your target audience's demographics, interests, pain points, and preferred communication channels. This knowledge will guide your content creation and influencer selection.

Develop a Content Strategy: Create a content strategy that aligns with your business goals and target audience. Determine the types of content you will create (e.g., blog posts, videos, podcasts), the topics that resonate with your audience, and the channels you will use to distribute your content.

Create Valuable and Engaging Content: Produce high-quality content that provides value to your target audience. Focus on educating, entertaining, or inspiring them. Incorporate relevant keywords to improve search engine visibility and optimize your content for social sharing.

Consistency and Frequency: Consistency is key in content marketing. Develop a content calendar to ensure a regular and consistent publishing schedule. This helps establish trust with your audience and keeps them engaged.

Amplify Your Content: Share your content through various channels, including your website, blog, social media platforms, email newsletters, and industry forums. Encourage your audience to share and engage with your content by including social sharing buttons and CTAs.

Identify Influencers: Research and identify influencers who have a significant following and influence within your target market. Look for individuals who align with your brand values and can authentically promote your products or services. Tools like BuzzSumo and social media platforms can help in finding relevant influencers.

Build Relationships with Influencers: Engage with influencers by following them on social media, commenting on their posts, and sharing their content. Cultivate genuine relationships by providing value, collaborating on content, and supporting their initiatives. Building strong relationships with influencers can lead to long-term partnerships.

Collaborate with Influencers: Propose collaboration opportunities to influencers such as guest blogging, social media takeovers, product reviews, or joint webinars. Ensure the collaboration aligns with the influencer's style and provides value to their audience. This collaboration helps extend your reach and tap into the influencer's engaged following.

Sponsored Content and Influencer Campaigns: Consider sponsoring influencer-created content or running influencer campaigns. This involves compensating influencers for promoting your brand or products. Ensure the content is authentic and resonates with the influencer's audience.

Measure Results and Optimize: Track the performance of your content and influencer collaborations. Monitor metrics such as website traffic, engagement, social shares, conversions, and brand mentions. Analyse the data to identify what's working and optimize your content and influencer strategies accordingly.

Foster User-Generated Content (UGC): Encourage your audience to create and share content related to your brand. Implement contests, hashtags, or encourage user reviews and testimonials. UGC serves as social proof, boosts engagement, and extends your brand's reach.

49 *Testimonials are great for generating customer confidence and also help with SEO. Crucial to have them to the fore.*

Monitor and Respond: Monitor mentions and conversations about your brand and influencer collaborations. Respond promptly to comments, questions, and feedback from your audience. This helps build trust and strengthens your brand's reputation.

By combining a strong content strategy with influencer collaborations, you can effectively market your business, increase brand visibility, and drive engagement and conversions. Remember to continuously measure your results, optimize your strategies, and adapt to evolving trends and preferences to stay ahead in the ever-changing marketing landscape.

TRADITIONAL ABOVE THE LINE MARKETING – DIRECT MAIL, TV, RADIO & MORE

Traditional above-the-line marketing refers to traditional advertising methods that are aimed at reaching a wide audience through mass media channels. These methods include direct mail, TV, radio, print advertising, and outdoor advertising. While digital marketing has gained significant popularity in recent years, traditional above-the-line marketing still plays a crucial role in reaching a broad target audience and building brand awareness. Let's explore these traditional marketing methods in more detail:

Direct Mail: Direct mail involves sending promotional materials such as postcards, brochures, or catalogues directly to potential customers' mailboxes. It allows businesses to target specific geographic areas or demographics. Direct mail can be highly personalized and offers a tangible experience for recipients. It can be effective in reaching a local audience and generating leads or driving sales.

Television Advertising: Television advertising allows businesses to showcase their products or services through commercials aired on television networks. TV ads can reach a large and diverse audience, making it suitable for broad brand awareness campaigns. However, it can be costly, and targeting specific demographics can be challenging. With the rise of digital video streaming, businesses can also consider advertising on popular streaming platforms.

Radio Advertising: Radio advertising involves promoting products or services through audio ads broadcasted on radio stations. It offers an effective way to reach a local or regional audience and can be a cost-effective option compared to television. Businesses can create engaging and memorable audio ads that resonate with listeners and drive them to take action.

Print Advertising: Print advertising includes placing ads in newspapers, magazines, trade publications, or other print media. It allows businesses to target specific audiences based on the publications they read. Print ads can be visually appealing and provide a longer-lasting impression compared to digital ads. However, it's important to consider declining readership in print media and evaluate the effectiveness of reaching your target audience through this channel.

Outdoor Advertising: Outdoor advertising, also known as out-of-home (OOH) advertising, involves placing ads in public spaces such as billboards, transit stations, bus stops, or on vehicles. It offers high visibility and exposure to a wide range of people. OOH ads can be particularly effective in reaching a local audience and creating brand awareness. Digital billboards have also emerged, allowing for dynamic and interactive advertising experiences.

Event Sponsorship: Sponsoring events allows businesses to showcase their brand and connect with a targeted audience. This can include sponsoring conferences, trade shows, sports events, or community gatherings. Event sponsorship provides opportunities for brand visibility through signage, banners, promotional materials, and engaging with attendees directly. It can help create positive associations with your brand and support community engagement.

Public Relations (PR): Public relations involves managing the spread of information about a business or brand through media channels. PR activities can include press releases, media interviews, press conferences, and organizing events. Traditional media coverage can significantly enhance brand visibility and credibility. Building relationships with journalists and influencers can help secure media placements and increase brand exposure.

Traditional Direct Marketing: Besides direct mail, traditional direct marketing methods include telemarketing, door-to-door sales, and print catalogues. Telemarketing involves making phone calls to potential customers to promote products or services. Door-to-door salespeople visit homes or businesses to sell products directly. Print catalogues allow customers to browse and order products via mail or phone. These methods can still be effective in certain industries or targeted geographic areas.

While digital marketing channels have expanded significantly, traditional above-the-line marketing methods continue to have their place in an integrated marketing strategy. The key is to understand your target audience, evaluate the reach and effectiveness of these methods, and determine how they fit into your overall marketing objectives. Combining traditional and digital marketing approaches can help maximize your brand's exposure and reach a diverse audience.

51

With traditional marketing companies under such pressure from Digital competition they will ALWAYS offer more if you are prepared to haggle. Put on the poor mouth and let them know you have only a small budget and you will be amazed at some of the reductions you will get. <u>Haggling is an art form!</u>

UTILISE INTERNAL STAFF FOR MARKETING TO KEEP COSTS DOWN

Utilizing internal staff for marketing can be a cost-effective strategy for businesses, particularly for small and medium-sized enterprises with limited budgets. By leveraging the skills and knowledge of existing employees, companies can save on hiring external marketing resources or agencies.

- Identify Employees with Relevant Skills: Assess the skills and expertise of your employees to identify individuals who have marketing-related skills or a keen interest in marketing. Look for employees with experience in areas such as graphic design, content creation, social media management, or copywriting. Capitalize on their talents and assign them marketing responsibilities. Assign someone to produce a company blog post every week and distribute on social media. This would be no more than 2 hours work.

- Provide Training and Development: Offer training and professional development opportunities to employees interested in marketing. This could include online courses, workshops, or seminars to enhance their skills and keep them updated with the latest marketing trends and strategies. Empowering employees with marketing knowledge can enable them to contribute effectively to your marketing efforts.

- Create Cross-Functional Teams: Foster collaboration between different departments within your organization. Encourage employees from various teams to work together on marketing initiatives. This approach brings diverse perspectives and expertise to marketing campaigns and ensures a well-rounded approach to reaching your target audience.

- Develop Internal Communication Channels: Establish internal communication channels, such as newsletters, intranets, or internal social media platforms, to share marketing updates and best practices with employees. Encourage employees to contribute ideas and suggestions for marketing campaigns. This creates a sense of involvement and ownership among employees and enhances their engagement in marketing activities.

- Encourage Employee Advocacy: Tap into the power of employee advocacy by encouraging employees to promote the company and its products or services through their personal networks and social media platforms. Provide them with relevant content, such as blog articles, infographics, or videos, that they can share with their connections. Employee advocacy can significantly amplify your brand's reach and credibility.

- Leverage Employee Networks: Employees often have their own networks and connections. Encourage them to participate in industry events, conferences, or networking opportunities where they can represent your company and promote its offerings. This can lead to valuable partnerships, collaborations, and business opportunities.

- Recognize and Reward Employee Contributions: Acknowledge and appreciate employees who actively contribute to marketing efforts. Recognize their achievements publicly, provide incentives or rewards for outstanding contributions, and create a culture that values and supports marketing initiatives. This encourages employees to continue engaging in marketing activities and motivates others to get involved.

- Monitor and Evaluate Results: Establish key performance indicators (KPIs) to measure the effectiveness of internal marketing efforts. Regularly review and analyse the results to identify areas of improvement and optimize your strategies. This data-driven approach helps you focus on initiatives that yield the best results and make informed decisions about resource allocation.

While utilizing internal staff for marketing can be cost-effective, it's important to strike a balance between leveraging existing resources and considering the need for specialized expertise. In some cases, outsourcing certain aspects of marketing, such as graphic design or search engine optimization, may still be necessary to ensure optimal results. The key is to assess your business needs, tap into the skills of your employees, and supplement with external resources when required.

> **52**
>
> *Engage Staff! Ask all of your staff to a meeting and get them to tell you what sort of hobbies and skills they have. See if they would like to help using some of these skills in their day job if there is a need. You will be surprised. You might have staff that do graphic design, web design, blog posts, social media etc and staff love to feel that they are an important cog in the wheel. Bringing staff with you as the company grows!*

CASE STUDIES

Case studies are an essential tool in marketing as they provide real-world examples of how a product or service has been successfully implemented and benefited customers. They offer a detailed analysis of a specific customer's experience, highlighting the challenges they faced, the solutions provided, and the outcomes achieved. So why are they so useful?

Demonstrating Value and Credibility: Case studies showcase the value and credibility of a product or service. They provide evidence of how the offering has positively impacted customers, solving their problems or fulfilling their needs. By presenting concrete examples of successful implementations, case studies build trust and confidence in potential customers, validating the claims made by the marketing messaging.

Addressing Customer Pain Points: Case studies delve into the specific challenges faced by customers and illustrate how the product or service effectively addressed those pain points. This helps potential customers relate to the problems being discussed and envision how the offering can provide a solution for their own challenges. Case studies act as powerful persuasion tools, showing the potential impact on customers' lives or businesses.

Building Trust and Social Proof: Consumers are more likely to trust the experiences and opinions of their peers than advertising messages from companies. Case studies serve as social proof by showcasing real customer success stories. They demonstrate that the product or service has been tried, tested, and proven effective by other customers, increasing trust and reducing scepticism.

Targeting Specific Industries or Niches: Case studies allow businesses to tailor their marketing efforts to specific industries or niches. By creating case studies focused on a particular industry, target audience, or customer segment, businesses can demonstrate their expertise and ability to solve industry-specific challenges. This targeted approach helps attract and engage potential customers who can directly relate to the case study.

Educating and Informing Customers: Case studies provide valuable insights and knowledge to potential customers. They demonstrate the capabilities and features of a product or service in a practical context, showing how it can be applied in real-life situations. This educates customers about the benefits and functionalities of the offering, helping them make informed decisions and understand the potential impact on their own businesses or lives.

53 Ask some of your best customers to participate in a case study

Differentiating from Competitors: Case studies can be used to highlight unique selling points and differentiate a product or service from competitors. By showcasing specific customer successes, businesses can emphasize their distinctive features, innovative approaches, or exceptional results. This helps position the offering as superior and preferable to alternatives in the market.

Supporting Sales and Conversion: Case studies serve as valuable sales enablement tools. Sales teams can leverage them during the sales process to demonstrate the value and benefits of the offering, address customer objections, and build trust with potential customers. Case studies provide concrete evidence that helps move prospects through the buyer's journey, ultimately increasing conversion rates.

Content Marketing and Thought Leadership: Case studies contribute to a company's content marketing strategy and thought leadership efforts. They provide valuable content that can be shared across various channels, such as websites, blogs, social media, and email campaigns. By consistently sharing case studies, businesses can establish themselves as industry leaders, showcasing their expertise and ability to deliver results.

Case studies are great for marketing as they provide tangible evidence of a product or service's value, address customer pain points, build trust, educate potential customers, differentiate from competitors, support sales efforts, and contribute to content marketing and thought leadership initiatives. Incorporating well-crafted case studies into marketing strategies can significantly enhance credibility, engage potential customers, and drive business growth.

CUSTOMER LOYALTY

Building customer loyalty is crucial for long-term business success. Loyal customers not only make repeat purchases but also become brand advocates, referring others to your business and providing positive reviews and testimonials. Here are some strategies to build customer loyalty:

1. Provide Exceptional Customer Service: Delivering exceptional customer service is a fundamental pillar of building loyalty. Train your employees to be friendly, attentive, and responsive to customer needs. Resolve issues promptly and go the extra mile to exceed customer expectations. A positive customer service experience creates a lasting impression and fosters loyalty.

2. Build Personal Connections: Make an effort to know your customers on a personal level. Use customer relationship management (CRM) systems to track preferences, purchase history, and communication preferences. Address customers by their names, send personalized messages, and tailor offers based on their interests. Building personal connections creates a sense of value and strengthens loyalty.

3. Offer a Superior Product or Service: Providing a superior product or service is crucial for gaining customer loyalty. Ensure your offering meets or exceeds customer expectations in terms of quality, functionality, and value. Continuously improve your product or service based on customer feedback and market trends to stay ahead of competitors.

4. Implement a Customer Loyalty Program: Develop a customer loyalty program to reward and incentivize repeat business. Offer exclusive discounts, rewards points, or special perks to loyal customers. Make the program easy to understand and use and communicate the benefits effectively to customers. A well-designed loyalty program encourages customers to choose your business over competitors.

5. Foster Engagement and Communication: Engage with your customers through various channels, such as social media, email newsletters, and blogs. Encourage feedback, respond to inquiries, and seek their opinions on new products or initiatives. Regularly communicate with your customers to keep them informed and connected to your brand.

6. Provide Value-Added Content and Education: Share valuable content, such as informative blog posts, how-to guides, or industry insights, that educates and benefits your customers. Establish yourself as a thought leader in your industry by providing relevant and helpful information. This positions your brand as an authority and enhances customer loyalty.

54 *Reward loyal customers. They can become great marketeers and evangelists.*

7. Seek and Act on Customer Feedback: Actively seek feedback from your customers to understand their needs and preferences better. Conduct surveys, online reviews, or feedback forms to gather insights. Analyse the feedback and make improvements based on the suggestions received. Show customers that you value their opinions and are committed to enhancing their experience.

8. Build Emotional Connections: Emotional connections play a significant role in building customer loyalty. Create positive emotional experiences by delivering surprises, personalized gestures, or acts of kindness. Show empathy and compassion in customer interactions, and make customers feel appreciated and valued. Emotional connections deepen loyalty and foster long-term relationships.

9. Encourage Referrals and Advocacy: Satisfied customers can become your most powerful marketing tool. Encourage them to refer friends and family to your business by offering referral incentives or rewards. Engage with loyal customers to become brand advocates by providing them with exclusive access, inviting them to share testimonials or participate in case studies. Their positive word-of-mouth can significantly impact customer loyalty.

10. Continuously Improve and Innovate: Finally, strive for continuous improvement and innovation. Stay abreast of industry trends, customer preferences, and competitive landscapes. Adapt and evolve your products, services, and strategies to meet changing customer needs and exceed their expectations. By consistently delivering value and staying ahead, you build trust and loyalty.

Building customer loyalty is an ongoing process that requires consistency, dedication, and genuine care for your customers. By prioritizing exceptional customer service, personal connections, value-added experiences, and continuous improvement, you can create a loyal customer base that supports your business's growth and success.

EXERCISE – IDENTIFY 3 x CUSTOMER REFERRAL SCHEMES FOR YOUR BUSINESS

HUSTLE

Finally, I want to explore the importance of hustle in all aspects of running a business but particularly in marketing.

1. Marketing is a fast-paced industry that requires quick thinking, adaptability, and the ability to stay ahead of trends. Hustling allows marketers to respond promptly to changes in the market, consumer behaviour, and emerging technologies. It enables them to seize opportunities and drive results in a competitive landscape.

2. Marketing is ultimately about achieving measurable results, whether it's increasing brand awareness, generating leads, driving conversions, or improving customer engagement. Hustle is crucial in taking action, implementing strategies, and executing campaigns that deliver tangible outcomes. It involves going the extra mile to meet deadlines, exceed targets, and constantly strive for success.

3. Hustling in marketing involves actively building and nurturing relationships with customers, stakeholders, influencers, and partners. It means going beyond the basic marketing activities to engage with the target audience, listen to their feedback, and provide personalized experiences. Building strong relationships helps create brand loyalty and advocacy, which leads to long-term success.

4. Marketing requires innovative and creative thinking to stand out in a crowded marketplace. Hustling involves constantly seeking new ideas, experimenting with different approaches, and pushing boundaries to find unique solutions. It means being proactive in exploring new marketing channels, technologies, and strategies to drive innovation and stay ahead of the competition.

5. The marketing landscape is continuously evolving, with new platforms, tools, and techniques emerging regularly. Hustle involves a commitment to continuous learning and self-improvement. Marketers need to stay updated with industry trends, consumer insights, and best practices. By being proactive in expanding their knowledge and skillset, marketers can deliver better results and drive business growth.

6. Hustling in marketing means taking initiative and being proactive in identifying opportunities and solving problems. It involves taking ownership of projects, seeking feedback, and taking calculated risks. Marketers who hustle are not afraid to try new strategies, pivot when needed, and take bold actions to drive success.

7. Hustle is essential in capturing and maintaining audience attention and engagement. It involves creating compelling

content, developing impactful campaigns, and optimizing marketing channels for maximum reach and impact. Marketers who hustle understand the importance of consistent and meaningful interactions with their audience to build brand loyalty and drive conversions.

 **Always be prepared to go the extra mile to get the deal done. Maybe not 'fake it till you make it', but a good entrepreneur needs to be able to box smart.**

8. In a dynamic marketing environment, things can change rapidly. Hustle enables marketers to stay agile and adaptable, ready to adjust their strategies and tactics to align with shifting market conditions or consumer preferences. It means being quick to respond to feedback, data, and insights, making necessary adjustments, and optimizing campaigns for better results.

9. Marketing is not without its challenges. From budget constraints to competition and changing consumer behaviour, marketers face various obstacles. Hustle involves resilience, determination, and a positive mindset to overcome these challenges. It means finding creative solutions, learning from failures, and continuously pushing forward to achieve marketing objectives.

The ability to hustle plays a vital role in marketing by driving action, achieving results, building relationships, fostering innovation, and adapting to changing circumstances. Marketers who hustle are more likely to succeed in a dynamic and competitive marketing landscape.

56 *FOCUS ON HAVING A GREAT PRODUCT OR SERVICE. This should contribute hugely to sales as it will help acquisition as your reputation grows and also help reduce churn over time.*

NOTES

CHAPTER
6

A SYSTEMATIC APPROACH

A SYSTEMATIC APPROACH TO business is vital for keeping on top of things. It refers to the implementation of organized and structured processes, methodologies, and frameworks to manage and operate a business. It involves developing clear strategies, establishing efficient workflows, documenting procedures, and is key for the following reasons.

- A systematic approach ensures consistency and standardization across various aspects of the business. By defining and implementing standardized processes, procedures, and guidelines, you create a uniform and predictable experience for customers, employees, and stakeholders. Consistency builds trust, improves efficiency, and reduces errors or variations in outcomes.

- A systematic approach lays the foundation for scalability and growth. It enables businesses to replicate successful processes and workflows, allowing for expansion into new markets, increased production capacity, or the addition of new products or services. Systematic approaches provide a framework that can be easily adapted and replicated as the business grows.

- Implementing systematic processes improves efficiency and productivity. By eliminating unnecessary steps, automating repetitive tasks, and optimizing workflows, businesses can reduce waste, minimize errors, and increase output. A systematic approach helps identify bottlenecks and inefficiencies, allowing for continuous improvement and enhanced productivity.

- Systematic processes contribute to risk mitigation and compliance with regulatory requirements. By documenting and following standardized procedures, businesses can ensure adherence to legal, ethical, and industry-specific guidelines. This helps minimize the risk of non-compliance, penalties, reputational damage, and other adverse consequences.

- A systematic approach provides a structured framework for decision making and problem solving. By gathering relevant data, analysing information, and following established processes, businesses can make informed decisions and effectively address challenges. Systematic approaches enable businesses to evaluate alternatives, assess risks, and select the most appropriate course of action.

- Systematic processes facilitate collaboration and communication within the organization. When everyone understands the established procedures and workflows, it becomes easier to coordinate efforts, delegate tasks, and ensure effective teamwork. Clear communication channels and standardized documentation foster transparency and alignment across departments and teams.

- A systematic approach directly impacts customer satisfaction and experience. By implementing consistent processes, businesses can deliver reliable and high-quality products or services. Customers appreciate predictability, timely delivery, and seamless interactions, leading to increased satisfaction and loyalty. Systematic approaches enable businesses to meet customer expectations consistently.

- A systematic approach fosters a culture of continuous improvement. By establishing processes that are regularly reviewed, businesses can identify areas for enhancement and innovation. Systematic approaches encourage feedback, data analysis, and learning from experiences, leading to ongoing refinement and optimization of operations.

- Systematic processes promote accountability and enable performance measurement. By defining roles, responsibilities, and key performance indicators (KPIs), businesses can monitor progress, track results, and evaluate individual and team performance. A systematic approach allows for effective performance management and goal alignment.

- Systematic approaches make businesses more adaptable and resilient. By developing agile processes, businesses can respond to changing market dynamics, technological advancements, or customer demands. Systematic approaches facilitate the identification of emerging trends and enable timely adjustments to stay competitive and relevant.

57 *Develop a systematic approach to work. I am a firm believer that you can apply the same skills and systems to different businesses in different verticals.*

CRM SYSTEMS

We have looked at CRM systems in Chapter 4 but as it is a core system we will look again in summary. A Customer Relationship Management (CRM) system is crucial to most businesses because it helps manage and streamline interactions with customers throughout the entire customer lifecycle. Some of the benefits include:

1. Centralized Customer Data: A CRM system serves as a centralized database for all customer-related information, including contact details, purchase history, communication history, preferences, and interactions across various channels. Having a single source of truth allows businesses to gain a holistic view of their customers, enabling personalized interactions and better decision-making.

2. Improved Customer Engagement: CRM systems provide tools for effective customer engagement. They enable businesses to track and manage customer interactions, such as phone calls, emails, and social media conversations, ensuring consistent and timely responses. With access to customer data, businesses can tailor their marketing and sales efforts to target specific customer segments, leading to more meaningful engagement.

3. Sales and Pipeline Management: CRM systems often include features for managing sales processes and tracking sales pipelines. They allow businesses to capture leads, track opportunities, and monitor the progress of deals. By providing insights into sales activities and forecasting, CRM systems help businesses optimize their sales strategies and enhance revenue generation.

4. Enhanced Customer Service: A CRM system enables efficient customer service by providing support agents with a complete view of a customer's history and interactions. Agents can access relevant information quickly, resolve issues promptly, and provide personalized support. This improves customer satisfaction, strengthens relationships, and increases the likelihood of repeat business.

5. Data-driven Decision Making: CRM systems offer robust reporting and analytics capabilities, allowing businesses to derive actionable insights from customer data. By analysing customer behaviour, preferences, and trends, businesses can identify opportunities for cross-selling, upselling, and customer retention. These insights enable data-driven decision-making to improve overall business performance.

When considering a CRM system for a small business, it's important to look for solutions that are affordable, easy to use, and scalable. Check out the examples of CRM systems we have looked at previously.

Remember, the best CRM system for a small business depends on specific requirements, budget, and integration needs. It's essential to evaluate different options and choose a CRM system that aligns with the business's goals and growth plans.

58 *CRM Systems are usually key for managing the sales process in most businesses*

INVOICING

Invoicing is a crucial aspect of managing and running a business. It ensures that you get paid for your products or services and helps maintain financial records. In today's digital age, there are various platforms available that simplify and streamline the invoicing process. Let's look at some:

1. QuickBooks: QuickBooks is one of the most widely used accounting software platforms that offers robust invoicing features. It allows you to create customized, professional-looking invoices, track payments, and automate recurring invoices. QuickBooks also integrates with bank accounts, making it easy to reconcile payments and generate financial reports.

2. Xero: Xero is another popular cloud-based accounting software that includes comprehensive invoicing capabilities. With Xero, you can create professional invoices, track due dates, and send automated payment reminders. It also offers features like online payment options, invoice templates, and the ability to set up recurring invoices.

3. FreshBooks: FreshBooks is a user-friendly invoicing platform designed for small businesses and freelancers. It offers customizable invoice templates, time tracking, expense management, and online payment options. FreshBooks also allows you to automate late payment reminders and send professional-looking invoices via email or traditional mail.

4. Zoho Invoice: Zoho Invoice is a simple and affordable invoicing platform that provides a range of features for small businesses. It allows you to create professional

invoices, track expenses, manage customer contacts, and accept online payments. Zoho Invoice also integrates with other Zoho productivity tools, making it a comprehensive solution for small business invoicing needs.

5. Wave: Wave is a free accounting platform that offers invoicing features suitable for small businesses and freelancers. It allows you to create professional invoices, customize templates, and track payments. Wave also integrates with payment gateways, enabling customers to pay invoices online. Although Wave is free, some advanced features may require a paid subscription.

6. PayPal: PayPal is a well-known online payment platform that also provides invoicing capabilities. With PayPal, you can create and send professional invoices, track payments, and accept credit card payments. PayPal's invoicing features are particularly useful for freelancers and small businesses that primarily conduct online transactions.

7. Square: Square is a popular point-of-sale (POS) system that offers invoicing capabilities for businesses. It allows you to create and send invoices, track payments, and accept online payments. Square also integrates with other Square tools like their payment processing system and inventory management, providing a cohesive solution for businesses.

8. Invoice2go: Invoice2go is a mobile invoicing app that allows you to create and send invoices on the go. It offers customizable invoice templates, payment tracking, and integration with various payment gateways. Invoice2go is suitable for small businesses, contractors, and service providers who need a simple and mobile-friendly invoicing solution.

These are just a few examples of the platforms available for invoicing. When selecting an invoicing platform for your business, consider factors such as your business size, invoicing needs, budget, and integration capabilities with other tools or software you use. Take advantage of free trials or demos to evaluate different platforms and choose the one that best suits your invoicing requirements. A well-chosen invoicing platform can save you time, improve accuracy, and enhance your overall financial management processes.

CASHFLOW

Improving cash flow is crucial for the financial health and stability of a business. Personally I have never been involved in a business where it was not under constant consideration. Here are some strategies you can implement to improve it:

1. Invoice promptly and follow up on payments: Send out invoices promptly after delivering products or services. Clearly state the payment terms and due dates. Follow up on late payments with friendly reminders and have a systematic process in place for managing collections.

2. Offer incentives for early payment: Encourage customers to pay their invoices promptly by offering incentives such as a small discount for early payment. This can incentivize customers to settle their invoices quickly and improve your cash flow.

3. Negotiate favourable payment terms with suppliers: Extend payment terms with your suppliers to optimize

your cash flow. Negotiate longer payment terms or request discounts for early payment. This can help manage your cash outflows and provide more flexibility in meeting your financial obligations.

4. Control expenses: Review your expenses regularly and identify areas where you can reduce costs. Look for cost-saving opportunities without compromising the quality of your products or services. This can free up cash and improve your overall financial position.

5. Tighten credit terms and conduct credit checks: Evaluate the creditworthiness of potential customers before extending credit to them. Consider implementing stricter credit terms, such as shorter payment windows or requiring deposits. Conducting credit checks can minimize the risk of late or non-payment.

6. Utilize cash flow forecasting: Develop a cash flow forecast to gain better visibility into your future cash position. This will help you anticipate any cash shortages and plan accordingly. By identifying potential gaps in advance, you can take proactive measures to address them, such as securing additional financing or adjusting your spending.

7. Optimize inventory management: Excess inventory ties up valuable cash. Regularly review your inventory levels and identify slow-moving or obsolete items. Consider implementing just-in-time inventory management practices to reduce inventory carrying costs and improve cash flow.

8. Explore financing options: In times of cash flow strain, explore financing options to inject capital into your business. This can include traditional bank loans, lines of credit, invoice financing, or business credit cards. However,

it's important to carefully evaluate the terms and costs associated with each option.

9. Implement effective cash management practices: Implement cash management practices to optimize your cash flow. This includes monitoring and managing your cash conversion cycle, negotiating favourable terms with your bank, and utilizing tools for cash flow tracking and analysis.

10. Improve sales and marketing efforts: Increasing sales can have a direct impact on your cash flow. Invest in effective sales and marketing strategies to attract new customers, retain existing ones, and drive revenue growth. This can include implementing targeted marketing campaigns, improving customer experience, and exploring new sales channels.

11. Invoice at stages. For example, if starting a project maybe invoice 50% upfront and do not start until payment is made. Then issue the final invoice at completion and do not handover until the invoice is paid. You can tell the client these are the terms at the outset. It takes discipline but believe me it can be transformative.

 **59** *Cash is King. I have seen many businesses go bust over the years as they did not have proper cashflow and collections systems in place. Really key to have this tied down*

Improving cash flow requires a combination of efficient financial management, effective collections, expense control, and proactive planning. By implementing these strategies, you can enhance your cash flow position and ensure the financial stability of your business.

PROJECT MANAGEMENT

Effective project management is crucial for ensuring the successful completion of tasks, meeting deadlines, and achieving project goals. There are several platforms available that can streamline project management processes, enhance collaboration, and improve overall efficiency.

1. Trello: Trello is a highly visual and intuitive project management platform that uses boards, lists, and cards to organize tasks. It allows you to create project boards, add tasks or cards, assign team members, set due dates, and track progress. Trello provides a simple and flexible interface that is suitable for small to medium-sized projects.

2. Asana: Asana is a comprehensive project management tool that offers features such as task management, project timelines, team collaboration, and progress tracking. It allows you to create projects, assign tasks, set priorities, and establish dependencies. Asana also integrates with other tools, such as communication platforms and file-sharing services, to streamline workflows.

3. Jira: Jira is a popular project management platform primarily used for software development projects. It provides robust features for issue tracking, agile development, and team collaboration. Jira allows teams to create and track tasks or issues, manage sprints, and generate detailed reports. It is widely used in the software development industry.

4. Basecamp: Basecamp is a project management platform that focuses on team communication and collaboration. It offers features such as task management, file sharing, messaging,

and scheduling. Basecamp provides a centralized space for teams to work together, share updates, and stay organized.

5. Microsoft Project: Microsoft Project is a powerful project management software that offers advanced features for planning, scheduling, and resource management. It allows you to create Gantt charts, allocate resources, track progress, and generate detailed reports. Microsoft Project is suitable for complex projects with multiple dependencies and resource constraints.

6. Monday.com: Monday.com is a versatile project management platform that offers customizable workflows and templates. It provides features for task management, team collaboration, and project tracking. Monday.com allows teams to visualize project progress, assign tasks, communicate, and integrate with other tools.

7. Wrike: Wrike is a cloud-based project management platform that offers a wide range of features for planning, task management, collaboration, and reporting. It provides a flexible interface, customizable workflows, and automation capabilities. Wrike is suitable for teams of all sizes and industries.

8. Smartsheet: Smartsheet is a collaborative work execution platform that combines project management features with spreadsheet functionalities. It offers features for task management, resource planning, reporting, and automation. Smartsheet allows teams to create and manage projects, track progress, and collaborate in real-time.

9. Teamwork: Teamwork is a project management platform that focuses on collaboration and task management. It provides features for project planning, time tracking,

document management, and communication. Teamwork offers a user-friendly interface and integrates with other tools to streamline workflows.

10. Airtable: Airtable is a flexible project management platform that combines the functionalities of spreadsheets and databases. It allows you to create custom project trackers, assign tasks, collaborate, and visualize project progress. Airtable is highly customizable and can be adapted to various project management needs.

When selecting a project management platform, consider factors such as the size and complexity of your projects, the needs of your team, ease of use, integration capabilities, and cost. Evaluate different platforms through trials or demos to find the one that aligns with your project management requirements and enhances your team's productivity and collaboration.

CMS SYSTEMS FOR A SMALL BUSINESS WEBSITE

Content Management Systems (CMS) are essential for small business websites as they offer numerous benefits in terms of website management, content creation, and scalability. Some of the benefits of a good CMS:

Easy Content Management: CMS systems provide a user-friendly interface that simplifies the process of creating, editing, and publishing content. You don't need technical expertise or coding knowledge to update your website. With a CMS, you can easily add new pages, upload images and videos, and format content using intuitive editing tools.

Quick Website Updates: CMS systems allow real-time updates, enabling you to make changes to your website instantly. Whether it's updating product information, publishing blog posts, or modifying contact details, you can quickly and efficiently keep your website content up to date. This agility is crucial for small businesses to respond to market trends and customer demands promptly.

Content Organization and Structure: CMS systems provide features like categories, tags, and search functionality that help organize and structure your content. You can categorize blog posts, products, or services, making it easier for visitors to navigate and find relevant information. Well-organized content enhances user experience and improves search engine optimization (SEO).

Customization and Design Flexibility: CMS systems offer a wide range of templates and themes that allow you to customize the look and feel of your website. You can choose from various design options, colour schemes, and layouts to create a unique and professional website that reflects your brand identity. Some CMS platforms also offer drag-and-drop interfaces, making it easier to rearrange elements and create custom page layouts without coding.

Multi-user Collaboration: CMS systems enable multiple users to collaborate on website management. You can assign different roles and permissions to team members, allowing them to contribute to content creation, editing, and publishing. This collaborative environment streamlines workflow, enhances productivity, and ensures consistent website updates.

SEO Optimization: CMS systems often include built-in SEO tools or plugins that help optimize your website for search engines. You can easily add meta tags, optimize URLs, and manage keywords to improve your website's visibility in search engine results. CMS platforms also provide SEO-friendly website structures and responsive design, which are essential for ranking well in search engines.

Scalability and Growth: CMS systems are designed to accommodate the growth of your business. As your small business expands, you can add new pages, products, or functionalities to your website seamlessly. CMS platforms offer scalability and flexibility, allowing you to adapt and meet the evolving needs of your business without significant technical challenges.

Examples of popular CMS systems suitable for small business websites include:

1. WordPress: WordPress is one of the most widely used CMS platforms, known for its user-friendly interface, extensive plugin ecosystem, and customizable themes. It offers a range of features suitable for small business websites, from simple blogs to e-commerce stores.

2. Joomla: Joomla is another popular CMS platform that provides flexibility and scalability. It offers a robust set of features, including content management, e-commerce capabilities, user management, and multilingual support.

3. Drupal: Drupal is a powerful CMS platform favoured by organizations with more complex website requirements. It offers advanced customization options, scalability, and security features. Drupal is suitable for small businesses

that anticipate significant growth and require a more robust CMS.

Remember to consider your specific website needs, technical capabilities, and budget when selecting a CMS system for your small business. Evaluate different options, explore their features and support, and choose a CMS platform that aligns with your goals and long-term website management requirements.

WHERE TO HIRE CONTRACT WEBSITE DEVELOPERS OR DESIGNERS AT REASONABLE PRICES

There are several popular marketplaces and platforms available for hiring contract website developers. These platforms provide a pool of talented professionals, allowing you to find the right developer for your specific project requirements. Here are some notable marketplaces you can consider:

1. Upwork: Upwork is one of the largest freelancing platforms, offering a wide range of web development services. You can post your job requirements and browse through the profiles of freelancers specializing in web development. Upwork provides tools for managing contracts, tracking work progress, and facilitating communication.

2. Freelancer: Freelancer is a global freelancing platform that connects businesses with web developers and other professionals. You can post your project, review proposals,

and hire freelancers based on their expertise and previous work. Freelancer provides features like milestones and escrow payment to ensure project completion and security.

3. Toptal: Toptal is a talent marketplace that focuses on connecting businesses with top-tier freelance developers. Toptal has a rigorous screening process, accepting only the top 3% of applicants, ensuring high-quality talent. They offer developers specializing in various web technologies and provide project management tools to facilitate collaboration.

4. Guru: Guru is a platform that connects businesses with freelancers across different industries, including web development. You can browse through freelancer profiles, review portfolios, and communicate directly with potential hires. Guru offers workroom collaboration tools and a secure payment system.

5. PeoplePerHour: PeoplePerHour is a freelance marketplace that allows you to post projects and receive proposals from web developers. The platform offers hourly or fixed-price projects and provides tools for managing work, tracking progress, and making secure payments.

6. Codeable: Codeable is a marketplace specifically focused on WordPress development. If you're looking for experienced WordPress developers for your website project, Codeable is a platform worth considering. Codeable vets and approves developers, ensuring their expertise in WordPress development.

 **60** *Marketplaces are great for hiring contract workers, particularly website & mobile app development and graphic design.*

7. 99designs: While primarily known for graphic design, 99designs also offers web development services. If you need both design and development work for your website, you can launch a design contest or hire individual developers through their platform.

When using these marketplaces, it's important to carefully review each developer's profile, portfolio, and feedback from previous clients. Take the time to communicate your project requirements clearly and discuss timelines, deliverables, and pricing before finalizing the contract. It's also a good practice to interview and evaluate potential developers to ensure they have the necessary skills and experience for your specific website development needs.

BUSINESS MEETINGS

YOU NEED AGENDAS AND ACTION POINTS

Setting agendas and creating action points are crucial for effective business meetings.

- Focus and Direction: Agendas provide structure and clarity to meetings. They outline the topics to be discussed, the goals to be achieved, and the order of discussion. By setting an agenda, you ensure that everyone is aware of the meeting's purpose and what needs to be accomplished. This helps participants stay focused and prevents the meeting from veering off track.

- Time Management: Agendas help manage meeting time effectively. By allocating time slots to each agenda item, you can ensure that discussions are efficient and that all important topics are covered within the allotted time. Clear time frames also encourage participants to come prepared and contribute to the discussion promptly.

- Preparation and Participation: Agendas provide an opportunity for participants to prepare in advance. By sharing the agenda beforehand, attendees can gather relevant information, think through topics, and come prepared with their insights and contributions. This promotes active participation, leading to more meaningful discussions and decision-making during the meeting.

- Accountability and Follow-up: Action points are specific tasks or actions assigned to individuals during the meeting. By documenting action points, you create a clear record of responsibilities and expectations. This promotes accountability among team members as they are aware of the tasks they need to complete. Additionally, action points serve as a basis for follow-up discussions and progress tracking in subsequent meetings.

- Decision-making and Problem-solving: Agendas help drive decision-making processes during meetings. By structuring discussions around specific topics or decisions to be made, agendas provide a framework for evaluating options, gathering input, and reaching conclusions. This ensures that important decisions are not delayed or overlooked.

- Communication and Alignment: Agendas serve as a communication tool, ensuring that all meeting participants are aligned on the topics to be discussed. By sharing the agenda in advance, attendees can provide input or request additional agenda items if needed. This promotes transparency, collaboration, and helps avoid surprises during the meeting.

- Meeting Effectiveness and Efficiency: Overall, agendas and action points contribute to the overall effectiveness and efficiency of business meetings. They help streamline discussions, keep participants on track, promote engagement, and ensure that meetings result in actionable outcomes. This ultimately saves time, enhances productivity, and maximizes the value of the meeting for all participants.

Remember to share the agenda with participants before the meeting, allowing them time to review and prepare. During the meeting, make sure to follow the agenda, manage time effectively, and assign clear action points. After the meeting, distribute meeting minutes or a summary that includes the discussed topics, decisions made, and assigned action points for future reference and accountability.

 **61** *Meetings are a waste of time unless action points are set, and people are responsible for delivering on these*

STAFFING

Is it better to hire staff or subcontract?

Whether it is better to hire staff or subcontract depends on several factors, including your business needs, the nature of the work, budget constraints, and long-term goals. Let's consider the advantages and considerations for each option:

Hiring Staff:

1. Control and Integration: Hiring staff allows you to have direct control over the work and integrate team members into your organization's culture and processes. They become a part of your team and can contribute to the growth and development of your business.

2. Dedicated Resources: Having dedicated staff members means they are solely focused on your business. They can develop a deep understanding of your operations, build long-term relationships with clients, and contribute to the success of your organization.

3. Flexibility and Adaptability: Staff members can be more flexible and adaptable to changing business needs. You can train them in specific areas, assign them to various projects, and easily reallocate resources as required.

4. Confidentiality and Intellectual Property: With in-house staff, you have more control over the confidentiality of sensitive information and intellectual property. You can implement security measures and internal policies to protect your business assets.

Considerations for hiring staff include increased overhead costs (salaries, benefits, office space, equipment), legal and administrative responsibilities (payroll, taxes, compliance), and the need for recruitment, training, and management.

Subcontracting:

1. Specialized Skills and Expertise: Subcontracting allows you to access specialized skills and expertise that may not be available within your staff. You can find experts in specific fields or niche areas, enabling you to deliver high-quality work and meet client demands.

2. Cost Efficiency: Subcontracting can be cost-effective, especially for short-term or project-based work. You can avoid the expenses associated with hiring and maintaining a full-time staff, such as salaries, benefits, and overhead costs. Subcontractors are typically responsible for their own expenses.

3. Scalability and Flexibility: Subcontracting provides flexibility to scale resources up or down based on project demands. You can engage subcontractors for specific projects or periods, reducing the need to maintain a permanent workforce during slower periods.

4. Reduced Administrative Burden: Subcontractors are responsible for their own administrative tasks, including taxes, insurance, and compliance. This can reduce the administrative burden on your organization.

Considerations for subcontracting include potential challenges in communication and coordination, reliance on external parties for timely deliverables, and the need for clear contractual agreements to protect your interests.

Ultimately, the decision between hiring staff and subcontracting depends on your specific business circumstances and goals. In some cases, a combination of both approaches might be appropriate. It's important to assess the specific requirements of your projects, consider your budget, evaluate the availability of skills in the market, and weigh the long-term implications before making a decision.

62 *Hiring can lead to all sorts of headaches particularly in early-stage startups. When building it is worth looking at sub-contracting where possible unless it is a key position*

CUSTOMER SUPPORT – WHY IS IT CRITICAL?

If you are in the service industry you will live or die on the back of your customer support. It is critical that you have the right systems in place as they can radically reduce workload whilst at the same time hugely improve customer satisfaction and loyalty.

Customer support is critical to most businesses and can help imrove many variables;

1. Customer Satisfaction and Retention: Excellent customer support plays a crucial role in ensuring customer satisfaction. When customers receive timely and effective

support, their issues and concerns are addressed, leading to higher levels of satisfaction. Satisfied customers are more likely to remain loyal, make repeat purchases, and recommend your business to others. On the other hand, poor customer support can result in customer frustration, negative experiences, and loss of business.

2. Brand Reputation and Image: Customer support significantly impacts your brand's reputation and image. When customers have positive interactions with your support team, it reflects positively on your brand. Conversely, negative experiences with customer support can damage your brand's reputation, leading to negative word-of-mouth, online reviews, and a tarnished image. Providing excellent customer support helps build trust and strengthens your brand's reputation in the market.

3. Competitive Advantage: In today's competitive business landscape, customer support can be a differentiating factor. Businesses that offer exceptional support and go the extra mile to assist their customers stand out from the competition. Excellent customer support becomes a competitive advantage, attracting and retaining customers in a crowded marketplace.

 **63** *Aim to exceed customer expectations when it comes to Customer Support. It will pay off as you scale.*

4. Increased Customer Loyalty and Lifetime Value: Strong customer support fosters customer loyalty. When customers feel valued and supported, they are more likely to remain

loyal to your business. Loyal customers tend to have higher lifetime value, meaning they make more purchases over an extended period. By investing in customer support, you can nurture long-term relationships with customers, increasing their lifetime value and ultimately driving revenue growth.

5. Feedback and Improvement Opportunities: Customer support provides valuable insights and feedback about your products, services, and overall customer experience. By actively listening to customer queries, concerns, and suggestions, you gain insights into areas that require improvement. This feedback loop helps you identify trends, identify pain points, and make necessary adjustments to enhance your offerings and address customer needs more effectively.

6. Crisis Management and Damage Control: When issues or crises arise, customer support plays a critical role in managing the situation. Responsive and empathetic customer support can help mitigate the impact of negative events, resolve issues promptly, and rebuild customer trust. Effective crisis management through customer support can help minimize the long-term consequences of a challenging situation.

7. Upselling and Cross-selling Opportunities: Customer support interactions provide opportunities for upselling and cross-selling. Well-trained support agents can identify customer needs, recommend relevant products or services, and generate additional revenue. By delivering personalized and helpful support, customer support teams can contribute to upselling and cross-selling efforts.

It's important for businesses to invest in the training and development of their customer support teams, provide the necessary tools and resources, and continuously monitor and improve the support process. By prioritizing customer support, businesses can foster customer satisfaction, loyalty, and long-term success.

CUSTOMER SUPPORT SOFTWARE SOLUTIONS

There are several software solutions available to help businesses streamline and enhance their customer support processes. These software solutions provide features and functionalities to manage customer inquiries, track support tickets, automate responses, and improve overall customer service. Here are some common types of software solutions for customer support, many of which I have used over the years:

1. Help Desk Software: Help desk software centralizes customer inquiries and support tickets, allowing businesses to track, manage, and respond to customer issues effectively. It provides features like ticket management, email integration, knowledge base management, and reporting. Examples of help desk software include Zendesk, Freshdesk, and Kayako.

2. Customer Relationship Management (CRM) Software: While primarily focused on managing customer relationships, CRM software often includes customer support features. It allows businesses to store customer information, track

customer interactions, and provide personalized support. CRM software with customer support capabilities includes Salesforce Service Cloud, Zoho CRM, and HubSpot Service Hub.

64 *Knowledgebase software allows you to build a searchable database of customer queries you have previously solved. It can become a manual of sorts. Other customers can then search this, reducing the inbound support calls and emails.*

3. Live Chat Software: Live chat software enables real-time communication between businesses and customers. It allows customers to chat with support agents directly on the website, resolving inquiries promptly. Live chat software may include features like chat routing, canned responses, file sharing, and visitor tracking. Examples include LiveChat, Intercom, and Olark.

4. Ticketing Systems: Ticketing systems provide a structured approach to managing customer support tickets. They allow businesses to categorize, prioritize, assign, and track tickets through various stages of resolution. Ticketing systems may integrate with other customer support tools or operate as standalone solutions. Examples include Jira Service Management, Help Scout, and TeamSupport.

5. Self-Service and Knowledge Base Software: Self-service software empowers customers to find answers to their questions independently. It includes knowledge base management systems, FAQs, community forums, and online

documentation. Self-service software reduces support ticket volume and provides customers with resources for self-help. Examples include Confluence, Zendesk Guide, and Freshdesk Knowledge Base. I have extensively used knowledgebase platforms such as Freshdesk. Every time you solve a customer issue simply add it to your knowledgebase and other users can search for the fix reducing the strain on support.

> **65** **Live Chat is great for lead generation and Customer Support. You can leave the same Live Chat plug in running on a website front end for sales enquiries and your Customer Support channel.**

6. Social Media Management Tools: Social media management tools help businesses monitor and manage customer interactions on social media platforms. These tools allow businesses to track mentions, respond to customer inquiries, and manage social media conversations effectively. Examples include Sprout Social, Hootsuite, and Buffer.

7. Voice and Call Centre Software: Voice and call centre software provide features to manage phone-based customer support. They include call routing, call recording, interactive voice response (IVR), and call analytics. These solutions help businesses handle high call volumes efficiently and ensure quality customer interactions. Examples include Five9, Avaya, and Genesys Cloud.

When selecting customer support software, consider factors such as the specific needs of your business, scalability, integration capabilities with existing systems, ease of use, reporting and analytics features, and the level of customer support provided by the software vendor. It's important to choose software that aligns with your business requirements and supports your customer support goals effectively.

THE DREADED TO-DO LIST

Let me start by saying I cannot function without a to-do list. That said I know there are plenty of people that manage fine without them. Horses for courses I suppose. Keeping it objective then if I can, why keep one?

Keeping a to-do list is generally considered a good practice for business and personal productivity. So why is maintaining a to-do list beneficial?:

1. Organization and Prioritization: A to-do list helps you stay organized by capturing and structuring tasks in one place. It allows you to see all your pending tasks, deadlines, and priorities at a glance. By organizing your tasks, you can prioritize them based on their importance and urgency, ensuring that you focus on the most critical activities.

2. Task Management and Time Allocation: A to-do list helps you manage your tasks effectively. By breaking down larger projects into smaller, actionable tasks, you can plan your time more efficiently. It allows you to allocate specific time slots for each task and estimate how much time you need for completion. This helps prevent tasks from slipping through the cracks and assists in meeting deadlines.

3. Productivity and Focus: A to-do list helps you maintain focus and avoid distractions. It serves as a reminder of what needs to be done, keeping you on track and reducing the likelihood of forgetting important tasks. By having a clear list of tasks to accomplish, you can prioritize your work and maintain productivity throughout the day.

4. Stress Reduction: A to-do list can alleviate stress and overwhelm by providing a sense of control and clarity. It helps you break down complex projects into manageable steps, making them feel more achievable. Crossing off completed tasks from the list also gives a sense of accomplishment, boosting motivation and reducing stress.

5. Accountability and Progress Tracking: A to-do list acts as a record of your commitments and progress. It helps hold you accountable for completing tasks and meeting deadlines. By tracking your progress and ticking off completed tasks, you can measure your productivity and identify areas for improvement.

6. Collaboration and Delegation: To-do lists can be useful for collaborating with team members and delegating tasks. They provide a transparent overview of project responsibilities, allowing team members to align their efforts and work together effectively. To-do lists can also facilitate communication and provide clarity on who is responsible for each task.

However, it's important to note that the effectiveness of a to-do list depends on how it is used. Here are a few considerations to ensure your to-do list is helpful:

- Keep the list manageable: Avoid overwhelming yourself with an excessively long list. Focus on the most important tasks to maintain clarity and avoid feeling overwhelmed.

- Regularly review and update: Review and update your to-do list regularly to reflect changing priorities, completed tasks, and new additions. This helps you stay up to date and adjust your plans accordingly.

- Be realistic with time estimates: When allocating time for tasks, be realistic about how long each task will take. Overestimating or underestimating the time required can lead to inefficiencies and frustration.

- Use a format that works for you: Choose a to-do list format that suits your preferences and workflow. It could be a digital tool, a paper planner, or a task management app. Experiment and find what works best for you.

Ultimately, a to-do list can be a valuable tool for business organization, productivity, and task management. It helps you stay focused, prioritize effectively, and track progress. However, it's important to adapt your approach based on your individual needs and preferences to derive maximum benefit from using a to-do list.

TOOLS TO HELP WITH A TO-DO LIST

There are numerous software options available for keeping a to-do list:

1. Todoist: Todoist is a widely used task management app that allows you to create and organize tasks, set due dates and reminders, collaborate with others, and track your progress. It is available on various platforms, including web, mobile, and desktop.

2. Microsoft To Do: Microsoft To Do is a task management app that integrates with other Microsoft productivity tools. It offers features such as task organization, due dates, reminders, attachments, and syncing across devices. It is available on web, iOS, Android, and Windows platforms.

3. Any.do: Any.do is a versatile task management app that offers features like task creation, due dates, reminders, attachments, and collaboration options. It also integrates with popular calendar applications. Any.do is available on web, iOS, and Android.

4. Trello: Trello is a visual project management tool that uses boards, lists, and cards to help you organize tasks and projects. It provides a flexible and customizable way to track tasks, set due dates, add attachments, and collaborate with team members. Trello is available on web, iOS, and Android.

5. Asana: Asana is a comprehensive project management and task tracking tool that allows you to create and assign tasks, set due dates, add attachments, and communicate with team members. It offers various features for managing projects and workflows. Asana is available on web, iOS, and Android.

6. Google Tasks: Google Tasks is a simple and lightweight task management app that integrates with other Google products like Gmail, Google Calendar, and Google Keep. It offers basic features like task creation, due dates, and subtasks. Google Tasks is available on web, iOS, and Android.

7. Wunderlist: Wunderlist is a popular task management app known for its user-friendly interface and cross-platform availability. It allows you to create tasks, set due dates, add

reminders, collaborate with others, and sync across devices. Wunderlist is available on web, iOS, Android, and Windows platforms.

These are just a few examples of software solutions for keeping a to-do list. Each option has its own set of features, interfaces, and integrations. It's recommended to explore the features of each tool, try out their free versions or trial periods, and choose the one that best suits your preferences and workflow.

 **66** *Not for everyone but I find a To-Do list a must have!*

CHAPTER
7

BUSINESS DEVELOPMENT

GROWING A BUSINESS TAKES multiple skillsets from the ability to persist through to the tough times to pivoting if your initial business model is not working. This is maybe more about the grind than the hustle. You have taken your business to validation, maybe been through initial fundraising, product development etc and now it is about the shoe leather. That hard work. The grind. Setting out your medium and long terms goals and possibly getting your business to an exit!

Growing a business indeed requires multiple skill sets and adaptability to overcome challenges and seize opportunities. Lets explore two key skills: persistence and pivoting.

1. **Persistence:**

Persistence is crucial for business growth because it enables entrepreneurs to stay focused, motivated, and resilient in the face of obstacles. Here's how persistence contributes to business growth:

a. Overcoming Challenges: Building and growing a business involves facing numerous challenges, such as financial constraints, market competition, and operational hurdles. Persistence allows entrepreneurs to tackle these challenges head-on, find creative solutions, and persevere until they achieve their goals.

b. Learning from Failure: Failure is an inevitable part of entrepreneurship. However, persistent entrepreneurs view failures as learning opportunities rather than setbacks. They analyse their mistakes, make necessary adjustments, and continue moving forward, armed with newfound knowledge and experience.

c. Building Relationships: Business growth often relies on building strong relationships with customers, suppliers, investors, and partners. Persistence helps entrepreneurs develop and nurture these relationships over time, leading to customer loyalty, beneficial partnerships, and access to necessary resources for expansion.

d. Long-Term Vision: Growing a business requires a long-term perspective and the ability to stay committed to the vision, even during challenging times. Persistent entrepreneurs remain focused on their goals and are willing to invest the time, effort, and resources necessary to achieve sustainable growth.

2. **Pivoting:**

Pivoting refers to the ability to change your business strategy or direction when the initial model is not yielding the desired results. Here's why pivoting is essential for business growth:

a. Adaptation to Market Dynamics: Markets are dynamic and ever evolving. Sometimes, the initial business model may not resonate with customers or fail to capture a viable market. By recognizing the need for change and pivoting, entrepreneurs can adapt to market demands, seize emerging opportunities, and position their business for growth.

b. Customer-Centric Approach: Pivoting often involves listening to customer feedback, analysing market trends, and identifying gaps or emerging needs. By pivoting, entrepreneurs can align their offerings more closely with customer preferences, improving customer satisfaction, and driving business growth.

c. Maximizing Resources: Pivoting allows entrepreneurs to optimize the use of resources. It may involve reallocating resources, repositioning the product or service, or entering new markets. By making strategic shifts, businesses can maximize the potential of their resources and improve overall performance.

d. Agility and Innovation: Pivoting requires a mindset of agility and innovation. By embracing change and experimenting with new ideas, entrepreneurs can uncover innovative solutions, differentiate themselves from competitors, and open up new avenues for growth.

It's important to note that persistence and pivoting are not mutually exclusive but rather interconnected. While persistence is essential for weathering challenges and staying the course, knowing when and how to pivot can be a strategic move that drives business growth. Successful entrepreneurs strike a balance between persistence and adaptability, leveraging their resilience to navigate tough times while being open to change and seizing new opportunities.

REMEMBER - BUSINESS IS NOT PERSONAL

On a serious note, this is one of the key learnings that only comes about through experience. When starting out in business, you cannot be blamed for taking everything personally. Things will go wrong. Products may fail. Clients may not pay their bills. Losses my accrue. You may have friends or family that may be reliant on you. You may have investors. Very often the CEO is the face of the business and the key driver of everything.

When things do go wrong, and they will, the stress caused by such situations can have devastating effects and in times like that you really need to stand back, take strength from friends and family and be as objective as possible. Shit will hit the fan! I doubt there is a successful founder that hasn't had to deal with some major adversity along the road and these indeed are often formative events. A true entrepreneur will always get back up on the horse!

THE SALES FUNNEL

We have covered this already in Chapter 4 – Sales, but it is key for growth. A sales funnel is a systematic process that guides potential customers through various stages of the buying journey, from initial awareness to making a purchase. It helps businesses capture leads, nurture them, and convert them into paying customers. By implementing a well-designed sales funnel and continually refining it, businesses can accelerate their growth and maximize their sales potential. As such it is key for business development. Please refer back to Chapter 4

KNOW YOUR CUSTOMER PROFILE

Knowing your customer profile is crucial for several reasons:

1. Targeted Marketing: Understanding your customer profile helps you tailor your marketing efforts and messages to effectively reach your target audience. By knowing their demographics, interests, preferences, and needs, you can create targeted marketing campaigns that resonate with your customers, increasing the chances of capturing their attention and converting them into loyal customers.

2. Product Development: Knowing your customer profile helps inform product development and innovation. By understanding their pain points, desires, and expectations, you can develop products or services that specifically cater to their needs. This customer-centric approach increases the likelihood of creating offerings that meet customer requirements and lead to customer satisfaction and loyalty.

3. Effective Communication: Understanding your customer profile enables you to communicate effectively with your customers. By knowing their preferred communication channels, language style, and communication preferences, you can tailor your messages to resonate with them. This improves the chances of capturing their attention, conveying your value proposition, and fostering meaningful engagement.

4. Customer Experience: Knowing your customer profile helps you enhance the overall customer experience. By understanding their preferences, you can personalize

interactions, customize offerings, and provide a seamless experience across various touchpoints. This personalized approach improves customer satisfaction, builds trust, and increases the likelihood of repeat business and positive word-of-mouth referrals.

5. Targeted Sales and Customer Acquisition: Knowing your customer profile enables you to focus your sales efforts on the right target audience. By identifying the characteristics and behaviours of your ideal customers, you can prioritize your sales efforts and allocate resources effectively. This targeted approach increases the efficiency of your sales process, leading to higher conversion rates and improved customer acquisition.

6. Competitive Advantage: Understanding your customer profile gives you a competitive edge in the market. By having a deep understanding of your target audience, you can differentiate your offerings, tailor your marketing strategies, and position your business more effectively against competitors. This understanding allows you to meet customer needs more effectively, stand out in the market, and attract and retain customers.

7. Business Growth and Sustainability: Knowing your customer profile is crucial for business growth and long-term sustainability. By understanding your customers' evolving needs, preferences, and behaviours, you can adapt your strategies and offerings to stay relevant and competitive in the market. This customer-focused approach helps drive business growth, foster customer loyalty, and ensure the longevity of your business.

Understanding your customer profile provides valuable insights that inform marketing strategies, product development, customer experience efforts, and sales approaches. It enables you to tailor your efforts to meet customer needs, enhance customer satisfaction, and gain a competitive advantage in the market, ultimately leading to business growth and success.

MINE YOUR CUSTOMER BASE – ALWAYS BE SELLING

Mining your customer base is a topic we again have already covered in Chapter 4 – Sales. It is though something that is also key for business development and as such it warrants a second mention here. Particularly when it comes to customer retention, upselling and identifying trends.

1. Customer Retention: Mining your customer base helps identify patterns and trends that contribute to customer retention. By analysing customer behaviour, preferences, and purchase history, you can identify loyal customers, understand their needs, and develop strategies to keep them engaged and satisfied. This insight can inform personalized retention efforts and customer loyalty programs, leading to increased customer loyalty and reduced churn.

2. Upselling and Cross-Selling Opportunities: Understanding your customer base allows you to identify upselling and cross-selling opportunities. By analysing their purchasing patterns, preferences, and demographics, you can identify products or services that complement their existing

purchases. This insight helps you tailor your sales and marketing efforts to promote relevant offerings, increasing the potential for additional sales and revenue generation.

3. Identifying Trends and Market Opportunities: Mining your customer base provides insights into broader market trends and opportunities. By analysing purchase patterns, preferences, and behaviour, you can identify emerging trends, shifts in customer preferences, and market demands. This information allows you to proactively adjust your strategies, identify new market segments, and capitalize on untapped opportunities.

Mining your customer base is an ongoing process that requires leveraging data analytics tools, customer relationship management (CRM) systems, and other technologies to extract actionable insights. By continually analysing and utilizing your customer data, you can make informed decisions, enhance customer experiences, and drive business success.

67 **Never underestimate the value you can extract from your existing customer base**

PARTNERSHIPS AND SYNERGIES - WHERE THERE IS A WIN WIN SITUATION TO BE HAD

Partnering and forming synergistic relationship with other companies can offer numerous benefits to help grow your business. Some of the key benefits include:

1. Access to New Markets and Customers: Partnering with companies that have an established presence in target markets allows you to tap into their customer base and gain access to new markets. This expands your reach and exposes your products or services to a wider audience, potentially increasing sales and market share.

2. Complementary Resources and Expertise: Partnering with companies can provide access to additional resources and expertise that you may not have in-house. This can include technological capabilities, specialized knowledge, distribution networks, or manufacturing facilities. Leveraging these resources can help you accelerate growth, improve operational efficiency, and enhance competitiveness.

3. Shared Costs and Risk Mitigation: Collaborating with partners allows you to share costs and mitigate risks associated with business growth initiatives. By pooling resources, such as marketing budgets or research and development expenses, you can pursue joint ventures or

strategic projects that might be otherwise unaffordable or too risky to undertake alone.

4. Synergistic Product or Service Offerings: Partnering with companies that offer complementary products or services can create synergies and enhance the value proposition for customers. By bundling or integrating your offerings, you can provide comprehensive solutions that address broader customer needs, increasing customer satisfaction and loyalty.

5. Market Expansion and Diversification: Partnering with companies can help you expand into new markets or diversify your customer base. By collaborating with companies in different industries or geographic regions, you can leverage their market knowledge, distribution channels, and customer relationships to penetrate new markets or target different customer segments.

6. Innovation and New Business Opportunities: Partnering with innovative companies can foster collaboration, idea-sharing, and the exploration of new business opportunities. By combining your expertise and resources with those of your partners, you can engage in joint research and development efforts, co-create new products or services, or explore emerging technologies and trends.

7. Branding and Reputation Enhancement: Partnering with reputable and established companies can enhance your brand image and credibility. Associating your brand with trusted partners can instil confidence in customers and stakeholders, opening doors to new business opportunities and strengthening your market position.

8. Competitive Advantage: Partnering with the right companies can give you a competitive edge in the market. By leveraging each other's strengths and resources, you can differentiate yourself from competitors, offer unique value propositions, and create barriers to entry for new market players.

It's important to note that successful partnerships require careful evaluation, mutual trust, and clear agreements to align goals and expectations. Effective communication, collaboration, and relationship management are essential to ensure the partnership's success and maximize the benefits for both parties involved.

68

Strategic partnerships are often a zero-cost solution for acquiring customers and in certain circumstances partnerships can add an underlying value to your business and it would not be uncommon for a partnership to lead to a sale or exit to the partner company

ALWAYS ADD VALUE WHERE POSSIBLE TO YOUR BUSINESS

Where you can, always be trying to add value. A business valuation is based on more than just revenue or profits. There can be considerable value in IP, in a customer opt in database, in business partnerships, recurring revenues, in brand awareness. ALL of these and more can have a $ value assigned to them and are things you should be aware of.

 *Always look to add value to your business. This helps to raise the valuation at any fundraising stage and exit.*

BUILDING IP

Building intellectual property (IP) in your business is important as it not only add $ value to the business but aids in a variety of ways:

- Competitive Advantage: IP can provide a significant competitive advantage by differentiating your business from competitors. It establishes a unique selling proposition and creates barriers to entry for others trying to replicate your innovations or offerings. IP assets, such as patents, trademarks, or copyrights, can help protect your business's ideas, inventions, branding, and creative works, giving you a distinct market position.

- Value Creation: Building IP can enhance the value of your business. Intellectual property assets can be valuable assets that contribute to the overall worth of your company. They can attract investors, increase the attractiveness of your business for mergers and acquisitions, and open opportunities for licensing or partnerships, generating additional revenue streams.

- Market Monopoly and Exclusivity: IP rights, such as patents, provide legal protection and exclusive rights to your inventions or innovations for a limited period. This exclusivity allows you to capitalize on your inventions without competition, potentially commanding higher prices or licensing fees. It gives you the freedom to operate in the market and prevents others from using or benefiting from your inventions without permission.

- Innovation and Research Advancement: Building IP encourages innovation and research and development (R&D) within your business. By protecting and investing in your IP, you create an environment that fosters continuous improvement, new discoveries, and creative solutions. It promotes a culture of innovation and positions your business as a thought leader in your industry.

- Brand Protection and Reputation: IP protection, such as trademarks, helps safeguard your brand identity, logos, slogans, and product names. It prevents others from using similar marks that may confuse customers or dilute your brand reputation. By protecting your brand, you maintain control over how your business is perceived, ensuring consistency and maintaining customer trust.

- Licensing and Collaboration Opportunities: Building IP can open doors to licensing or collaboration opportunities. Your IP assets can be licensed to other companies for a fee, generating additional revenue streams. It can also facilitate partnerships and collaborations with other businesses, allowing you to leverage their capabilities, resources, and distribution channels.

- Employee Retention and Recruitment: IP can play a role in attracting and retaining top talent. Employees often seek opportunities to work on innovative projects and contribute to the development of IP. Building a culture that values and protects IP can make your business an attractive destination for skilled professionals, fostering employee loyalty and engagement.

- Future Growth and Expansion: IP can fuel future growth and expansion. As you build a portfolio of protected IP assets, you can leverage them to introduce new products or services, enter new markets, or explore licensing or franchising opportunities. It provides a foundation for future business expansion and diversification.

It's important to note that building and protecting IP requires strategic planning, legal expertise, and adherence to IP laws and regulations. Consulting with intellectual property attorneys or specialists can help ensure that your IP assets are adequately protected and managed to maximize their value and potential benefits for your business.

ANNUAL RECURRING REVENUE

Annual Recurring Revenue (ARR) is an important metric used in business valuation for several reasons:

1. Predictability and Stability: ARR provides a measure of the predictable and stable revenue generated by a business on an annual basis. Unlike one-time sales or sporadic revenue streams, ARR represents the ongoing revenue from subscription-based or recurring revenue models. This predictability and stability are attractive to investors and potential buyers, as it indicates a reliable revenue stream that can be sustained over time.

2. Revenue Visibility: ARR provides visibility into future revenue streams. It demonstrates the contracted revenue that will be generated in the upcoming year or years, giving investors and buyers confidence in the business's future financial performance. This visibility can support decision-making, strategic planning, and financial forecasting.

3. Growth Potential: ARR is often used as an indicator of a business's growth potential. A higher ARR suggests that the business has a strong customer base and a scalable business model. It indicates that the business has successfully acquired and retained customers, leading to predictable and recurring revenue. This growth potential is an attractive factor for investors and buyers, as it signals the opportunity for continued expansion and increased valuation in the future.

4. Revenue Quality: ARR represents a high-quality revenue stream. Since it is based on recurring or subscription-

based revenue, it tends to have higher retention rates and customer loyalty. This type of revenue is less susceptible to market fluctuations or one-time sales spikes, providing a more stable and sustainable revenue base. The quality of the revenue is an important factor in business valuation as it indicates the business's ability to generate consistent cash flows.

5. Valuation Multiples: ARR is often used as a basis for valuation multiples in the software as a service (SaaS) industry and other subscription-based businesses. Valuation multiples, such as the price-to-earnings (P/E) ratio or price-to-sales (P/S) ratio, can be applied to a business's ARR to estimate its overall value. The higher the ARR, the higher the potential valuation of the business.

6. Investor and Buyer Interest: ARR is a metric that attracts investor and buyer interest. Investors and buyers are often looking for businesses with a strong recurring revenue base, as it provides more predictable returns on their investment. ARR acts as a key indicator of the business's financial health and potential profitability, making it an important factor in investment and acquisition decisions.

Overall, ARR provides valuable insights into the financial performance, growth potential, and stability of a business. It is a key metric used in business valuation, especially for companies with subscription-based or recurring revenue models. A higher ARR can contribute to a higher valuation, attracting investor interest and providing a measure of the business's future revenue potential.

70 *Try where you can extract residual annual income from your companies. It provides a strong asset value to your business and if you have low churn, is almost guaranteed income. All industries are trying this now. Even car manufacturers are looking to charge annual fees for 'services' and 'updates' like roadside assistance and navigation. BMW now charge a monthly fee for heated seats. Wrap your head around that ARR!*

SAAS

SaaS stands for Software as a Service. It is a software delivery model in which applications are hosted and provided to customers over the internet on a subscription basis. Instead of purchasing and installing software on their own servers or devices, customers access the software and its features through a web browser.

In the SaaS model, the software provider is responsible for hosting, maintaining, and updating the software infrastructure, while customers pay a recurring subscription fee to access and use the software. SaaS offerings often have a multi-tenant architecture, where multiple customers share the same infrastructure while their data and configurations are kept separate and secure.

The Annual Recurring Revenue (ARR) model is closely related to SaaS. ARR refers to the annualized revenue that a business expects to receive from its customers on a recurring basis. In the context of SaaS, ARR represents the contracted recurring revenue from subscription fees that the SaaS provider anticipates generating over the next year.

The SaaS business model is typically based on recurring revenue, where customers pay a subscription fee on a regular basis, such as monthly or annually. This predictable and recurring revenue stream is a key characteristic of SaaS businesses and is often a significant driver of their valuation.

ARR is a fundamental metric used to assess the financial performance and growth potential of SaaS businesses. It provides visibility into the annual recurring revenue that the SaaS provider can rely on and use for business planning, financial forecasting, and decision-making. ARR helps demonstrate the health and scalability of the business, as well as its ability to generate consistent cash flows.

Investors and buyers often use ARR as a key factor in valuing SaaS companies. The ARR model enables them to estimate the value of a SaaS business by applying valuation multiples to its annual recurring revenue. The higher the ARR, the higher the potential valuation of the SaaS company, as it indicates a strong customer base, predictable revenue, and growth potential.

Overall, SaaS and the ARR model are closely intertwined. SaaS businesses rely on recurring revenue generated through subscriptions, and ARR is a critical metric to measure and assess the financial performance and value of SaaS companies.

Valuing a SaaS (Software as a Service) business involves assessing its financial performance, growth potential, market position, and other factors. Several valuation methodologies are commonly used in the industry, including:

1. Revenue Multiple: This approach involves applying a multiple to the business's annual recurring revenue (ARR) or another revenue metric. The multiple can vary based on factors such as growth rate, profitability, customer retention, and market conditions. Typical revenue multiples for SaaS companies range from 3x to 10x or higher, depending on various factors specific to the business.

2. Earnings Multiple: Instead of focusing solely on revenue, this approach considers the company's profitability and applies a multiple to its earnings metric, such as EBITDA (Earnings Before Interest, Taxes, Depreciation, and Amortization). The multiple depends on factors such as growth rate, margin, risk profile, and industry benchmarks.

3. Customer Lifetime Value (CLTV) and Customer Acquisition Cost (CAC): This approach analyses the relationship between the value of a customer over their lifetime and the cost of acquiring that customer. By assessing CLTV and CAC, investors can estimate the business's growth potential, scalability, and long-term profitability.

4. Discounted Cash Flow (DCF): This valuation method estimates the present value of the business's future cash flows, considering factors such as revenue growth, profitability, capital expenditures, and the cost of capital. DCF analysis requires making assumptions about future performance and discounting those cash flows to their present value.

5. Market Comparables: This approach involves comparing the SaaS business to similar publicly traded or recently sold

companies in terms of revenue, growth rate, profitability, and other relevant metrics. Comparable transaction multiples or market capitalizations can serve as benchmarks for valuing the business.

It's important to note that valuing a SaaS business is complex, and different methodologies may yield varying results. The specific circumstances of the business, including its growth rate, market position, competitive landscape, and industry trends, should be carefully considered. Engaging professional valuation experts or advisors with experience in the SaaS industry can help ensure a comprehensive and accurate valuation.

VALUING A BUSINESS

Valuing businesses in different industries requires consideration of industry-specific factors and the application of appropriate valuation methodologies. A restaurant may for example be valued at 2 - 3 X EARNINGS whilst a SaaS business might be valued at 8 X ARR or more as the multiple tends to increase as the ARR increases. While the valuation process may vary depending on the industry, here are some general approaches that can be used:

1. Financial Performance Metrics: Evaluate the financial performance of the business by analysing its historical and projected revenue, profitability, cash flow, and other relevant financial metrics. Industry-specific benchmarks and ratios can be used to assess the company's performance relative to its peers.

2. Market Analysis: Conduct a thorough analysis of the industry in which the business operates, including market size, growth rate, competitive landscape, and market trends. Understanding the industry dynamics helps assess the business's position within the market and its potential for future growth and profitability.

3. Comparable Company Analysis: Identify comparable companies within the industry and analyse their financial metrics, market multiples, and transaction data. This approach involves comparing the target business to similar companies in terms of size, growth prospects, market share, and other relevant factors. Comparable company analysis can provide insights into the valuation of the target business.

4. Asset-Based Approach: Assess the value of the business's tangible and intangible assets. Tangible assets include physical property, equipment, and inventory, while intangible assets can include intellectual property, brand value, customer relationships, and proprietary technology. This approach is particularly relevant for asset-intensive industries.

5. Discounted Cash Flow (DCF) Analysis: Apply the DCF method, which estimates the present value of the business's projected future cash flows. This approach requires forecasting future cash flows, determining an appropriate discount rate to reflect the risk of the industry, and discounting the cash flows to their present value. DCF analysis is commonly used across industries and provides a comprehensive assessment of a business's intrinsic value.

6. Industry-Specific Metrics: Some industries may have unique valuation metrics or methodologies. For example, in the

technology sector, metrics like user growth, engagement, and customer acquisition costs may be important. In the healthcare industry, metrics such as patient volume, reimbursement rates, and regulatory factors may play a significant role in valuation.

It's crucial to note that industry-specific expertise and knowledge are important when valuing businesses in different industries. Engaging professional valuation experts or advisors with experience in the specific industry can help ensure accurate and reliable valuations tailored to the industry's characteristics and nuances.

71

Valuation. Be very careful when it comes to valuing your business. On many occasions I have seen businesses drastically undervalued by their founders particularly when they are looking for an exit due to tiredness, personal circumstances changing etc. It is invaluable to get some objective analysis and to develop a strategy to help sell for the maximum $$. You need to plan and strategize for an exit. Even if it is a quick one.

72 *LAST BUT NOT LEAST. Consider a Mentor or a non-exec Director. It is a great resource when it comes to fund raising, exit negotiations, business development and much more. A good Mentor or non-exec can also help to fast track growth and save huge $$ by helping with strategies and avoiding pitfalls. Experience can help to plug all sorts of holes and rapidly scale your business.*

29 QUICK TIPS

Let's finish up by summarising some of the more crucial tips with a few new ones for good measure!

73. **DO ONE THING REALLY WELL.** You can build a successful business in a niche once you focus on creating the best product or service you can. Indeed, you can often successfully operate in a niche within a niche. However all business owners will face distraction or temptations to develop new services or products as their business grows, but focus is key. Be better than the competition. A good product or service will sell itself and if you focus on delivering the best product you can, your customers will eventually become cheerleaders, advocates, marketeers and will be a key driver for sales as they spread the word amongst their networks.

73. Minimise your $ exposure. **SPEND AS LITTLE AS YOU HAVE TO UNTIL YOU HAVE SALES** – Even Company formation, legal etc can be done after you start selling.

74. Take a day away with no distractions to **WORK ON A BUSINESS PLAN.**

75. Take a day to **RESEARCH THE VARIOUS GOVERNMENT SUPPORTS.**

76. **DEVELOP A MARKETING STRATEGY**: Determine the most effective channels and tactics to reach your target market and create awareness about your business.

77. **NEVER ASSUME.** Assumption is the mother of all F*** Ups

78. Be sure that any potential customer you are dealing with is **THE DECISION MAKER**

79. **SPEND REASONABLE $$ TO BUILD AN ONLINE PRESENCE**: Create a professional logo, website, leverage social media platforms, and explore digital marketing strategies to expand your reach.

80. **PROVIDE EXCELLENT CUSTOMER SERVICE**

81. **ESTABLISH STRATEGIC PARTNERSHIPS**: Collaborate with complementary businesses to expand your reach, access new markets, and leverage each other's strengths.

82. **BUILD THE BEST TEAM YOU CAN**. Be self-aware; upskill and fill holes. Ideally have really key personnel with skin in the game OR leave a small equity pool for key staff hires.

83. **KEEP A SMALL EQUITY POOL FOR POTENTIAL KEY HIRES** into your business.

84. **GET DISCIPLINED**. Turn the phone off for X hrs to get work done. Schedule regular down time for reading, sport, family. Use a To-do list.

85. **CONSIDER A MENTOR OR NON-EXEC DIRECTOR**. Can fast track growth and help avoid speed bumps.

86. **IMPROVE YOURSELF - LEARN & READ**. Stay updated on industry trends, attend conferences or workshops, and invest in professional development to enhance your skills and knowledge.

87. **CHECK EMAIL AT MOST TWICE A DAY**. 12pm and 5pm

88. **TAKE PERSONAL RESPONSIBILITY.** When things do go wrong, I can assure you, that if you had prepared better, took better precautions, built something differently,

researched better, whatever it may be, the incident may not have happened. Unless you acknowledge this and take ownership of your mistakes you will never learn and grow. A person of good character will always take responsibility and own their mistakes

89. **RESEARCH YOUR MARKET**: Understand your target audience, industry trends, and competitors to identify opportunities and challenges.

90. **ALWAYS BE SELLING**. Build confidence socially. Always be prepared to talk to a total stranger and tell them about your business.

91. **FOCUS ON CUSTOMER NEEDS**: Prioritize delivering value to your customers and continuously seek feedback to improve your products or services.

92. **MANAGE YOUR TIME EFFECTIVELY**: Prioritize tasks, set clear goals, and establish routines to maximize productivity and avoid burnout.

93. **DEVELOP SYSTEMS** for sales, cashflow, invoicing, customer support and anything else relevant to your business.

94. **HUSTLE**. What business is all about. The ability to get the job done. Stay persistent and resilient: Entrepreneurship can be challenging.

95. **GRIND**. Get up an hour earlier every day. There is no substitute for hard work. DO NOT BE OUTWORKED

96. **PERSEVERENCE AND RESILIENCE** are key to overcoming obstacles and achieving long-term

success. Keep going. This is what for me separates true entrepreneurs from the chaff

97. **TAKE UP A HOBBY**. You need some distraction from work and family. A social hobby like Golf or hillwalking is great to clear the cobwebs and also can be great for networking

98. **BE GOOD TO YOURSELF**. You cannot look after your friends or family if you don't look after your self first

99. **MENTAL HEALTH**. In these stressful times try and incorporate some real downtime to help keep mental health in order. Some short yoga sessions, Wim Hoff deep breathing, mindfulness sessions, cold showers are some of the things I try and incorporate randomly into my week. You can really feel the dopamine hit after a cold shower

100. **ENJOY WHAT YOU DO**! For me being an entrepreneur is about freedom. If you have passion, then the revenue should follow.

NOTES

I hope this book will have been of some quantifiable value. Maybe help you avoid some pitfalls, save time, save money, ultimately help you get where you are going in a more direct fashion whilst not losing your home or your mind along the way. As the focus has been on clear and concise pointers and strategies, and these will change from one person to the next, I will finish up with 5 takeaways which have been most relevant on my journey;

Validation - For me the most crucial of steps when starting out. This will not always be possible but I highly recommend spending as little money as possible, never mortgage your home, avoid loans, gifts, investment if you can. Prove your business first, then fund raise to scale.

Develop a systematic approach to your business - Most of these skills will be transferable and over time you will improve your business savvy.

Focus on creating the best product and customer experience you can - This WILL pay off in the long term. If you have the best product, price becomes less of a consideration for the customer and likewise with excellent customer service and support your customers will become champions and marketeers for your business.

Take risk. But calculated risk - You need to be shrewd and know when to roll the dice. You can play it safe with a lifestyle business and there is nothing wrong with that, but many risk takers set out with lofty aims. On a personal note, I would never advise taking a business loan or investment money from family or friends. A red line for me.

Enjoy the ride - Set business targets. Hit those targets. Take up a hobby. A personal regret is that I didn't take up golf earlier. Cut the bullshit and bullshitters out of your life. Find some smart friends. Schedule time for family. Read. Reward yourself. If you are not good to yourself it is hard to be good to those you care about.

"Enjoy life. There's plenty of time to be dead."
— Hans Christian Andersen